SLICING THROUGH ADVERSITY

WITH FAITH, FIRE & FLOUR

JOE CARLUCCI

ISBN: Paperback: 979-8-9992055-0-6
E-Book: 979-8-9992055-1-3

Library of Congress: 2025912360

Printed in the United States of America

Cover design by Marie Stirk.

Find me at www.valentinaspizzeria.com

To my daughter,

You bore the weight of our hardships with a heart far too big for your years.

You stood beside me as we locked the doors on dreams, sold the furniture that held our memories, and even gave up your own bed—not with a complaint, but with courage.

In the silence of loss and the chaos of starting over, your love became my anchor, and your laughter, my light.

This book, this journey, every page of perseverance, is for you.

We didn't just survive.

We rose.

Love,
Dad

CONTENTS

Chapter One: The Family Business: Their Business, Our Family 1

Chapter Two: Carlucci's 21

Chapter Three: Making the Team 44

Chapter Four: The Marshal 64

Chapter Five: Famous Joe's 80

Chapter Six: Alabama 100

Chapter Seven: Tortora's 110

Chapter Eight: Madison, Alabama 121

Chapter Nine: The Decline of Famous Joe's and the Hustle Culture 133

Chapter Ten: Joe's World Famous 145

Chapter Eleven: Valentina's 156

Chapter Twelve: Valentina's 2.0 165

Chapter Thirteen: The Best of the Best 185

CHAPTER ONE

THE FAMILY BUSINESS
THEIR BUSINESS, OUR FAMILY

My pace has been the same for as long as I can remember. I've got one gear—GO. I've always been a hustler, even as a kid.

I have a deep aching in my bones to run at something full speed and keep running at it with an all-or-nothing mentality. When I achieved a goal, I'd look for the next goal to aim for and grow into.

This innate instinct, formed in the pit of my gut, created an unbreakable work ethic. It carried me from my first job as a nine-year-old boy in 1986 to running one of the best pizzerias in America.

Of course, when I was nine years old and working at the batting cages, getting paid in cash under the table, all I knew was that I had the best job in the world. I called myself the King of the Cages. It was a safe place to go without school tests or the embarrassment and stigma of my school performance.

School was hard for me. I needed help understanding

and learning as fast as the others in class. Back in the 1980s, nobody knew what ADHD was or that I had it. Teachers put me in smaller classes for a handful of subjects. I had to sit on a rug and was treated differently from my friends. Everyone knew those classes were *special.* I did what I could to move in and out of those classrooms without anyone seeing me. I had a core group of friends in childhood, and we stuck together. I accepted questions about my grades and why I was in the carpet classes from them, but not from anyone else.

My response was always the same: *Beats the hell out of me.*

The second the school bell rang, and I was released, I felt free. After school, I'd drop my bookbag off at home, run a few blocks down to the batting cages, and immediately start picking up balls. I'd race around and time myself from one ball to another. And when it was slow, I'd grab a bat and hit until someone else came. When the sun set and the street lights came on, my mom drove over to get me, and I'd leave for the night with some cash in my pocket.

Most of the neighborhood boys had gigs to occupy their free time. I'm sure our parents considered it more of a blessing that we had somewhere to go, so we weren't inside the house and in their business all the time. For me, it was a necessity. My home life wasn't stable. It felt better to be outside than inside.

Homes in my childhood neighborhood in Carmel, New York, an hour north of the Bronx, weren't anything to brag about. Our home was a typical two-story home on a street lined with two-story homes. We had four walls, a roof, and food in the fridge. Our kitchen was small, and considering my mom couldn't boil water to save her life, we never sat down as a family for mealtime. My sisters shared a room, and I had a tiny room lined with Michael Jordan and Yankee posters.

Like most in my neighborhood, my parents were hard-working. The bills got paid, as far as I knew, and I never really wanted for anything. My mom worked three jobs, and my dad was a salesman. From the outside, we looked like a typical family in the suburbs.

But I never saw the cops bust down the front door of any of my friends' homes, which made us stand out. My parents fought a lot, threw plates, screamed at each other, and neighbors often called the police for a domestic disturbance concern. When the cops arrived, I'd jump out a window and run.

I'd run as fast as I could, but some guy in blue would always catch me and take me home. The next day on the school bus was always uncomfortable. Everyone, including me, knew there was a problem at our home.

My parents divorced when I was in elementary school. It was better that way for everyone. My dad moved back to the Bronx but was often around. He showed up whenever my recreational basketball or baseball team had a game or my friends and I needed a ride to the mall. Most kids in the eighties and nineties needed rides to walk around the mall.

He'd drive for hours just to sit in a parking lot and wait for me. Sometimes he was forced to wait because he'd run out of gas and couldn't leave anyway.

As I grew up, I didn't just want to be out of the house. I wanted to make money doing it, and eventually traded in the freedom and fresh air of the batting cages for a part-time job at a department store. I didn't last long as a cashier because it wasn't stimulating or challenging for me at all. I had to stand in one place for an entire shift, doing the same thing for hours. The money was better than the batting cages, but it wasn't enough to satisfy me.

I checked the wanted section of the newspaper and saw that the hospital had a housekeeping position open. The pay was better, and I could do it after school. It didn't take more than a few shifts to recognize that it fulfilled me. I took on my role as a housekeeper with pride because it was something other people didn't want to do.

Every day was different. I never knew what I'd be asked to do when I showed up for my shift. It was an adventure. I had to stay alert because I'd get paged throughout my shift, which kept me on my toes.

Most people didn't want to do the job because the housekeeper had to clean up patients' rooms after accidents or spills, clean bathrooms, which was humbling, and scrub the morgue and operating rooms after surgeries. I'm sure others thought that part of the job was too creepy. I looked at every task as a challenge and did it to the best of my 14-year-old ability.

On the shifts where I'd be sent into operating rooms after surgery to clean up the mess left behind, I'd let my imagination run wild as I'd move a mop back and forth across blood-stained floors. I'd tell myself stories about what happened on the table, who the person was, and what brought them into the operating room.

On the days I had to clean the morgue, I found it thrilling. Some days, I was down there by myself. I wasn't scared of death. I'd seen too many horror movies in the eighties to be afraid of dark hallways, plus I wanted to excel at the job and keep it for as long as I could because it paid even more than the department store. So, I'd clean the room, pull back sheets, open up drawers, and take a peek. I didn't look for too long, but long enough.

I loved working there. I felt respected and seen. People thanked me for helping them, which lit me up. It didn't matter that I didn't get good grades or couldn't pass standardized state tests. When I put on the uniform for work and stepped inside the hospital, I felt loved and appreciated. For years, I worked a four-hour shift every weekend, both days.

When my mom got a job at a dry cleaner, she'd bring home pizza for dinner a lot from the pizzeria next door. One day, she noticed a sign in the pizzeria's window that they were looking for help. My mom got my sister a job at the pizzeria. Not long after, I followed too. I was hired as a dishwasher.

At first, the job wasn't all that stimulating, but the environment was exciting. Being Italian myself, I loved working with other Italians. I loved how they talked to each other and how fast they moved. My sister fell in love with one of the owners, and he looked out for me. He owned it with his brother. Their father was from Sicily. Even though he wasn't an owner, he showed up daily and made the sauce from scratch. It was just tomato sauce, but they treated it like gold.

He'd catch me looking at him working on it and shout, "Don't look at the sauce, kid."

It only took once, and that was it. I didn't look at the sauce, ask about it, touch it, or even think about breathing on it. I was pretty sure he'd seen a thing or two in his day and didn't want to get on his bad side. Or anyone's bad side, for that matter.

I'm sure it could have happened too. I wasn't stupid. I knew who the men in suits were when they came in for a meal. They didn't try to hide why they were at the pizzeria or whisper even. They'd greet me, nothing more than small talk. I'd respond, but I moved along quickly without looking curious or interested. I kept my head down and did what I was told.

The longer I worked there, the more I noticed nobody used a recipe. There weren't any hanging on the walls or stuck to the fridge, and there wasn't a binder or a safe filled with secret family recipes.

An order would come in, and a pizza maker would toss the dough and know the exact amount of sauce, cheese, and toppings, how long to cook the pizza, and when to turn it so that the pizza would be perfect every time. It was all muscle memory, and I wanted more from the pizzeria than just washing dishes. I wanted to be a pizza maker. That was my next goal, but it took me two years of working wherever they needed me and doing what I was told before I finally got the nerve to ask to be a pizza maker.

"One day," the owner said to me and patted my back.

I didn't push the matter. I let it be, but I watched with more intent.

Nobody ever measured flour. Whoever made the pizza would just rip open a bag of flour and dump it into a mixer. That was easy to remember. The water came from an old Italian ice bucket. Once the bucket was empty and washed out, the owner drew a line on the side of it with a marker. I was told to make sure the bucket was always filled to the line. The salt, sugar, yeast, and oil were all measured and weighed out, and then added to the flour and water mixture.

I didn't know the measurements or weight, but it seemed simple enough. Every once in a while, I'd imagine myself tossing pizza in the air. Once I got my driver's license, I got out from behind the dishes and became a delivery guy. I liked that much better. Every day was different. I never knew where I'd end up or who would answer the door.

And then, on a random day right before we closed for the night, I was told just to go make a pizza.

"Seriously?"

"Do I need to ask you twice?"

I ran into the kitchen, threw an apron over my head, and tied it quickly behind my back. I grabbed a tray of dough out of the refrigerator and just started pushing the dough out. I had no idea what I was doing. I tossed the dough the way I saw everyone else do it. I was surprised by how hard it was to stretch it.

"Holy shit, this is hard," I laughed and glanced up at the owner.

"You've got it," he said and nodded at me.

I stretched it to sixteen inches out, but couldn't get it very round. My hand started cramping, and the muscles in my forearms burned. I couldn't keep tossing or pushing. It wasn't getting any bigger. Adding the sauce looked easy, but doing it for the first time was a mess. I took a ladle of sauce and plopped it in the center of the dough and swirled it around in a circular motion from the center to the edge. It took a while for me to get it even. I grabbed a heap of cheese and threw it on, and then finished it with pepperoni. It was challenging, but I had fun doing it.

I grabbed a pizza peel, shoved it in the oven, and waited. I watched the clock, pacing in front of the oven, just waiting. After enough time went by, I opened the oven door and slid the peeler back under the crust. The owner came over to check out my pizza. We stood there looking at it, side-by-side, neither of us saying anything at first.

He patted me on the back.

"Not bad for your first time," he said enthusiastically. "How did it end up looking like a football?" I laughed.

"I don't know, kid. I've never seen anything like that before."

"Jesus," I sighed.

"Try it again next week after we close."

I looked forward to my practice pizza run all week. Tuesday came, and I couldn't wait for my shift to end. I watched the clock tick closer to closing time. I prayed that I didn't have another delivery and could jump in the back and try to make a pizza that didn't look like a football. I was hoping to get one closer to a circle.

As soon as the owner turned the open sign hanging in the door to close, I threw on an apron, washed my hands, and got to work.

I grabbed a tray of dough out of the refrigerator and just started pushing the dough out. I stretched it, tossed it, stretched it, tossed it, and kept doing it until my fingers started hurting. I pinched the edges, went lighter on the sauce, placed cheese around with intention, and added sausage and peppers on the second one. I picked up the side closest to the edge of the counter, slid the peeler under it, and placed it a bit further back in the oven. This time, I opened the oven door halfway through and turned it.

My second attempt was much better. It looked like I'd been doing it for years. It was oval, which was a big improvement, and the cheese melted more evenly.

The owner was preoccupied with something, so he didn't come over right away to check on me. I cut it up and had my first slice of a pizza I made by myself, without a recipe or any real instructions. It wasn't anything special. It was pizza—flour, salt, water, tomato sauce, I couldn't dare look at years before, cheese, sausage, and peppers. I'd deliver pizzas just like it time and time again. But standing there in the kitchen, I felt like I'd grown up a bit.

I made pizzas over and over again after hours for several weeks in a row. And then, the owner finally took me aside and showed me the art form and how to make the dough look like an actual pizza. I never got the title of full-time pizza maker. It was just one more way for me to work. Even then, I was allowed to try on different hats and roles.

I was hustling. If I wasn't at school, I was at the pizzeria or the hospital. If I wasn't at either of those places, I was at a third job I got at a nearby gym to have free membership. I didn't know what I wanted to be as an adult, but I knew I loved making money, staying fit, and keeping busy.

To graduate, I had to pass a state standardized test. And I couldn't do it. I took it several times and failed just as many. Finally, my mom fought for me to have extra time to take the test. The morning of my high school graduation came, and my mom called into the school to see if I was walking across that stage and getting a diploma. I prayed she'd get a big, fat yes. I could tell even before she got off the phone. I jumped around the house, screaming. I had never been more grateful for anything than I was at that moment. I graduated.

After that, I did what most good kids did in the nineties. Despite having no real direction in life, I went to college. I paid my way to a state university. Since my parents didn't bankroll college, I spent a year doing all the drugs I could and enjoying the brotherhood I established through the fraternity I joined. I loved that part of college. The fraternity was awesome. I didn't have older brothers as a kid, so having guys to look up to as a 20-something-year-old was reassuring.

But I knew deep down, the brotherhood I established wasn't enough of a reason to stay in college. I didn't want to waste any more of the hard-earned money I had been saving since I was nine, so I transferred to a community college forty minutes from my mom's house and got back my job at the hospital and pizzeria.

It didn't matter where I went to school. It didn't help shape me or point me in a direction I saw in terms of a career, even though I was working in two different industries and could have gotten full-time jobs at either. I left college and immediately felt shame from my mom. She was concerned that the neighbors would think less of us as a family because I couldn't finish college.

In the 1990s, suburban kids were expected to go to college, get a degree, make a lot of money, marry young, have babies, and die old. When I left school, I became the family's black sheep.

Maybe it's an Italian thing, but we've always been great at creating a tight-knit chosen family that exists beyond blood relatives. My family supported me and tried to help me find my place in life.

One of my sister's brothers-in-law got me a job at an electrical company. To accept it, I had to leave the hospital. I loved it there, but lost the passion for it. When I turned in my two-week notice, they begged me to stay. I was the top employee. I couldn't stay out of respect for my boss. I was lost and depressed. Not being able to fit into what society expected of a typical 19-year-old man weighed on me.

I worked for the electrical company for a year. I didn't want to keep bouncing around from job to job, but I felt a void and was waiting for the right opportunity to fill it.

One night, I was talking to a good friend from high school who worked for a national food manufacturer and distributor. He loved it. When he described his day, he had enthusiasm in his voice, and I felt a pang deep down in my gut. He sounded like he was having fun and enjoying what he did day after day. I missed that feeling. Like everyone, he had challenges, and he had to overcome obstacles on the fly, but every day brought on something different.

It didn't take me long to ask for an introduction. It turned out the company had an opening in its delivery department. I would get up at 2:00 a.m. and deliver potato chips throughout the Tri-State area. I'd finish at 11:00 a.m., and since that didn't work for the electric company, I took on more hours at the pizzeria. I was always tired—bone tired, scrambling, and rushing. I made mistakes occasionally, but I thrived under tight deadlines.

Everyone else was concerned about my long days. I wasn't. When I put pressure on myself, I was efficient and at my optimal performance. I took care of myself, ate a balanced diet, and exercised. I was happy and productive and felt like I had purpose again. But I understood why everyone else was worried about me. There's only so long a person can go on little sleep, long days, and busy highways.

By this point, my sister had married into the pizzeria. Her husband worked there, and his brother owned the place. It was all family to me, and my brother-in-law eventually offered me a full-time job at the pizza shop. To keep everything happy and even-keeled in the family, I left every other part-time job and worked day in and day out at the pizzeria. For years, life was the same day in and day out.

Finally, the owner approached me and said he wanted to open another location—this time in Danbury, Connecticut. I was eager and young, and when I heard the offer, my heart practically ripped out of my chest.

"I'll do it," I said, interrupting him. "Whatever you want, I'll do it."

"Let me finish, kid," he laughed.

"Right. Sorry, go ahead," I tried to calm myself down, but could barely contain myself. I heard bits and pieces of what he said next.

"You'll be a partner. You'll run it. And when it's paid off, it'll be yours on paper."

All I could think to say was, "When do I leave?"

"You'll have to work seven days a week."

"No problem."

"You'll be responsible for hiring and firing employees."

"I can do that."

"You'll pay all the bills but rent and food costs."

"Great."

And that was it. I packed up my life and couldn't wait to leave. More than that, I wanted just to get in and get started. I wanted to prove myself to everyone that I was going to *be* something and accomplish something great. Even if that meant I didn't have a college degree.

I was older and a little wiser than the last time I moved away from home. I was still in my mid-20s, and I wasn't a saint by any means. I rented a room from a friend who lived a few minutes down the road from the shop. We would go to bars and clubs and stay out till morning, but I had significantly more responsibilities than I did when I was at the state university and didn't want to mess up or disappoint my brother-in-law.

When I got to the new shop in Danbury, I felt a surge of excitement and just a little hint of anxiety. Of course, I didn't show that, though. As far as anyone would have guessed, I was the new kid in town and had my shit together.

The 1,500-square-foot shop was next to a significant movie rental business that had stores around the country. That was a big, fat checkmark in the pro column. But we had two in the con column.

It would have been the perfect location for a pizza shop, but there was a foul smell at night. It came from a plant nearby, and the owners sunk $200,000 into the small space, hoping the aesthetic would make up for the smell.

I was 24 years old and needed to learn how to hire the right people or manage a team. I put a Help Wanted sign out front, accepted applications, and interviewed people on the spot. If they had kitchen experience, and I felt good about them, I offered them a job. Within a week, I had hired a dozen people to work next to me.

Not long after that, we were ready to open the door to the public and start making money. I wouldn't leave the door open at night because of the smell. I wanted people to come in and smell pizza, not slaughter or processing machines downwind of the plant.

It was hard for video renters not to see the store, and we did get good foot traffic most nights. But I didn't want to rely on the chance the video rental place would be slammed, and we'd get a bunch of orders.

I became a scholar, and every minute I had free time, I dedicated myself to learning all I could about marketing and what other pizzerias around the country were doing to bring in customers.

I had guys standing out on street corners handing out flyers. We painted the storefront window with specials and deals. I sent pizzas to city official offices and influential people in the area.

And then one night, after work, I saw the Danbury Knights of Columbus was holding a Best in the City Pizza contest.

This is cool, I thought.

Pizzerias were invited to participate in an event held on a Saturday. We were asked to bring premade pizzas for attendees to try. They would go around the event space, getting to try ten different pizzas from local businesses and vote for their favorite.

My place was voted Best Pizza in the City for two years running! I was very proud of that. I sought out ways to bring in new business, and did it in a cheap but effective way. Every year that we were voted the best pizza around, I'd see a bump in sales. It was great for a few months, but eventually faded away.

One night in January, I was on the internet searching for new ways to promote against the big-name pizza brands everyone knows, when I saw an ad to try out for the US Pizza Team in Columbus, Ohio, that weekend, while competing in various pizza events. It was all happening at the Soft Serve & Pizza Show.

What's this about? I thought as I clicked the ad.

This was the first time I had heard of a pizza competition team, let alone pizza competitions. But there it all was—laid out for me to just say yes to.

I entered myself in all the competitions.

- **Fastest Dough**—The purpose of this competition was to see who could shape a certain number of doughs to stretch across pizza screens the fastest. The dough couldn't rip or have holes in it, and it had to fit a specific size.
- **Largest Dough**—Competitors were given the same allotted amount of time to toss and stretch a ball of dough, which all weighed the same and was as large as possible without ripping it.
- **Freestyle Acrobatic Pizza Tossing**—This was the

hardest one of them all. We all got balls of dough. We had to perform an acrobatic routine to music while shaping, stretching, and handling the dough into a pizza shape. We were judged on our tricks, level of difficulty, how many times we accidentally dropped the dough, and how well we performed to the music selected.

- **Pizza Box Folding**—This was fun. Everyone was given the same number of unassembled pizza boxes. When the judge said—3-2-1-Go, we'd rush like hell to fold all of them the quickest we could.
- **Best Pizza**—And after it's all said and done, we all want to be a champion of how our pizzas actually taste. There's no point in being the fastest slinger or someone who can stretch dough the biggest if the pizza itself tastes like shit.

Columbus was about ten hours away from me. I knew I had to do it. I asked a few friends to join me, so I had company on the ride and even at the event. After I closed up the shop that Saturday, we all met up at my place. I threw some clothes, put my pizza supplies in the back of my car, and got on the highway, heading west with some buddies. We took turns driving, going through the night, and stopping a few times in Pittsburgh to fill up on gas, energy drinks that tasted like battery acid, and use the bathroom. We made amazing timing and pulled into the arena parking lot around 8:00 a.m., right before the event opened up.

I was driving that last leg. The others got out to explore, but I leaned my chair back and was able to catch a few minutes of sleep in my car before checking in for the competition.

Tony Gemignani was the judge of the largest dough and acrobatics competitions. But he was the one who was also putting together the US Pizza Team. I heard of him but didn't know much more than he was a well-known pizzeria owner in California. He was already successful and wasn't able to compete anywhere anymore as an individual, so he wanted to create a competition team. Other countries had competitive teams. Tony wanted to hand-select who would be on his team.

After I checked in and got my badge, I walked around the show floor with my friends in absolute awe. We were sleep deprived, absolutely. But there was no denying the electricity in the room. The energy was incredible. As we made our way around the convention center, the cramped road trip melted away from my mind, and I was thrilled to be in that space. There were competition heats already happening, people throwing dough everywhere, and I was high on adrenaline.

I felt connected to a community for the first time since being shut out from my brother-in-law's pizzeria. Even more importantly, I felt inspired for the first time in even longer. It was easy to introduce myself to other pizza shop owners, competitors, and even vendors. I took it all in.

As we got closer to the back of the show floor, a loud voice filled the room. I saw a large man on stage entertaining the audience. I felt called to sit down and listen to him, and caught him in the middle of a story.

"How was I supposed to get ahead of my competitors if I didn't know what they were doing?" he asked his crowd.

He went on to say, "I had no choice," his hands up in the air. "I had to climb into the dumpster. There wasn't any other way!" His voice was compelling, his eyes were wide, and his smile was really welcoming.

The room erupted with laughter. I started laughing too. Whatever story this guy was telling was one I wanted to hear the end of. I leaned in and looked around the room, astounded that he had everyone engaged with him.

"At the end of the night, after they locked the door and turned off the lights, I'd sneak around back and dig through their trash. Yes, it was disgusting, but I had to do it. I ripped open a few bags, grabbed receipts, and stuffed as many of them as I could into my pockets. I got out of there as fast as possible, but you better believe I added those addresses to my direct mail database, and those folks got a nice coupon to my store the following week."

I have to meet this guy.

After his speech, I hung around to introduce myself to him. Most people did. It took him a while to make his way to the back of the audience section, where I was standing.

"Hi, I'm Joe," I said as I stuck my hand out for him.

"Dave."

He towered over me by at least eight inches. I've never been the tallest guy in the room, but I was never the shortest either. If I've got a shoe with a lift at all, I'm pushing 5'10", but usually I'm 5'9. This guy, who I learned was named Dave, had to be at least 6'6", 300 pounds. His hand engulfed mine as he reached out and shook it.

"I loved your story. I only caught that part of your talk, though," I laughed. "What do you do?"

"I'm a consultant and travel around speaking about how

to bring in new customers and get ahead of your competitors," Dave said, smiling ear-to-ear.

"You really did that. Did you climb in the dumpster?"

"When I had a restaurant, I did," he laughed.

I could tell he and I were going to be good friends. We walked and talked for a while. I told him about my shop in Danbury, getting the best pizza in the city two years running, and about the smell at night.

Dave and I exchanged numbers, and he went his way, and I went mine. I continued walking around the show floor until my time to compete in the largest dough heat came. I saw Dave talking to Tony, the judge.

I heard "3-2-1-Go," and I started working my dough as fast as I could. I had five minutes to stretch the dough as big as possible without it ripping.

I've got this. Easy.

I got the dough formed and was ready to toss it and stretch it. I was doing great, showing off, and feeling really confident in myself. I glanced at Tony, who was walking around looking at competitors' styles and techniques. He nodded at me and quietly said, "You got it. You don't have to do it anymore. Just stop."

I let that get to my head, and I thought, *oh yeah, watch this.*

I threw the pizza in the air one more time, and it ripped in half. And just like that, I was disqualified.

After my heat was over, Tony came up to me and told me that I should have listened to him. I was heading to Italy, and then my stupid arrogance and pushing it just one toss too far, I lost my spot.

The feeling was familiar. I had something good going, but I self-sabotaged.

I didn't place in the others either: best pizza, box folding competition, fasting dough or the acrobatic one. It was thrilling to be around guys who were clearly passionate about slinging dough, tossing it, beating their own personal record and winning.

I left the competition exhausted but hooked on the concept of making the US Pizza Team. As one of my friends drove, I researched Tony, and when I could try out again. I had to wait an entire year to try out in Ohio again, but there were tryouts in New York and Los Angeles. I read article after article about Tony.

He was a legend in the industry already.

Man, I should have listened to him.

He had been around the block in the pizza competition scene for years already. He'd won, and judged, and knew people everywhere. He didn't just make great pizza and wasn't already well-known around the world; he had a vision for the industry, and I wanted to be a part of it.

CHAPTER TWO

CARLUCCI'S

LIFE WENT ON AS NORMAL FOR A WHILE AFTER I LOST my chance to go to Italy with Tony and the US Pizza Team.

One day, the owners came into the store, and I assumed it was a friendly visit. They hadn't been out in some time, and I hadn't spoken to my brother-in-law in a while. I figured they were just checking on me and the place. But after we exchanged small talk, the top dog told me that the sales at my store weren't cutting it. I immediately went on the defensive because I saw the sales and made the pizzas myself. I knew we were moving as fast as we could, and we were selling a good number of pizzas. If we hadn't started $200,000 in the hole, our sales would have been fine. But because we had such a big gap to fill, the owners were unsatisfied.

I was stunned. My brother-in-law couldn't even look at me. "Joe, it's just not working," the owner said.

"So, what then? You're closing it?" I shouted, my hands up in the air.

The room was practically spinning, and my staff all got quiet and just watched us. "We want you to buy it from us," he said flatly.

I couldn't believe what he just said. I looked at them both, then at my staff, hoping to see the same look of surprise on their faces as I assumed was on mine.

"You want me to buy the store?"

"Yes. For the full $200,000."

I paced back and forth in front of them. I was pissed and confused. "Where do you think I'm going to get that kinda cash? It's not even worth that."

"You aren't going to buy it then?"

I stopped in my tracks, put my hands at my sides, and steadied myself. "No," I said sternly.

"Then give me the keys and get out. The rest of you have to go too," the owner said.

I took my apron off, threw the keys on the counter, grabbed what was mine from the back, and left without looking back. Everyone followed me.

"I'm sorry, you guys," I said as calmly as I could.

I assured the staff they would get paid for whatever time I owed them, and I'd keep in touch with them all.

I drove around for a while, trying to clear my head and figure out what I was going to do next. I couldn't go back home to New York. I felt betrayed by my family, who I believed knew that my brother-in-law's family was about to give me an ultimatum and never warned me. It came out of the blue, and I was blindsided. Even though I knew the pizzeria was involved with men in suits, I felt like I was their family. They loved me and always took care of me. To be kicked out on the street like that without so much as next month's rent was humiliating.

I wanted to work somewhere totally different. As luck would have it, it was the summertime, and there was a carnival in town that was hiring. Before going home, I drove the carnival, found the guy in charge, and asked if he was hiring.

Right then and there, I became his newest glorified babysitter, and I could start work on opening day. Training was easy.

Take tickets. Tear tickets.

Throw tickets away.

Don't let more than two kids go down the slide at the same time.

Repeat.

Simple, and I loved it. All I had to do was use my grown-up voice when kids didn't listen and collect a paycheck. It was easy work, and it paid my bills. And when the carnival moved one town over, I went with it. I was a carnival worker all summer long.

After my shift ended one night, I was in the kitchen making myself something to eat, and I heard a knock at the door. I looked through the peephole and saw two guys in suits. I knew who they were. I knew who sent them. And I knew pretending like I wasn't at home wasn't an option, so I opened the door just enough to see them both.

"Hey, Joe," one of them said, and I nodded. "Can you come outside and talk to us?"

I waited for them to take a step away from my door and nodded my head.

I followed them across the street to the parking lot. I

figured they weren't going to kill me in a parking lot, but I stayed alert and on edge. If they were going to pull a gun or knife on me, I was going to be ready. I looked around the parking lot for people. There was regular foot traffic, but I didn't see anyone I knew to call over to make an introduction. Witnesses were always a good sign that nobody was dying.

They stopped in the middle of the lot and turned toward me.

Here we go, I thought.

"You owe us money," one of them said.

I stood my ground, hands at my side, ready to defend myself or start throwing punches.

"I don't owe you anything. I paid the bills. I'm not buying the place for $200,000. I've said this before."

"This isn't finished," one of them said before getting into the car and driving away.

I watched them leave the parking lot before exhaling and running back upstairs into my apartment. My heart was pounding so hard I could hear it in my eardrums. I locked the door with all three locks—the deadbolt, and handle lock, and the chain.

I checked the window and didn't see them. It was hard to calm down. I paced back and forth for a few minutes, threw my lunch in the trash, and had to head out for my shift at the fair mall. I was grateful my job was pretty mundane and didn't require a lot of brain power. My thoughts were all over the place.

I was pissed that the men in suits came to my place. And I wondered if they'd be back later that night. And if not that night, when? They really thought I was responsible for the revenue hit the pizzeria took, even though they were the ones who sunk more money than they should have to renovate it. They were the ones who bought a place down the street from a processing plant that made the whole area smell like someone was burning sewage for hours.

I did what they asked of me. And I was good at it.

A few days later, I got a call from the owner. I was invited to the main shop to talk. They called it *a sit-down*. It was scheduled for the next day. I agreed, knowing that if I disagreed with them, the situation would only escalate, and I wanted to move on with my life.

The rest of the day crept by. I'd look at the clock every other minute, hoping hours passed in between glances. I did what I could to occupy my mind. I picked up a last-minute shift and exercised. A friend of mine called me that night to check in. He was taller, bigger, and stronger than I was. I told him what I was experiencing and what I had to do the next day. Gratefully, he insisted that he attend the meeting with me. I didn't argue. Having someone in my corner felt good.

The following day, I went about my regular routine. My friend came over and we got in my car with just enough time to spare. I didn't want to arrive too early, but not late either.

When I walked in, everyone was already waiting for me. Three men in suits were sitting at a table, along with the owner. The men in suits greeted me. The owner never even acknowledged me.

"Hello, Joey," one of the men in suits said.

"Joe," another one said.

"Hi, Joe," the third one said.

"Hello," I said back.

The men in suits pointed to a seat at a table that was next to them. I pulled the chair out at least two feet, giving myself plenty of space from the edge of the table and the men sitting around it. My friend hung back behind me. Nobody addressed him.

This time, they didn't encourage me to buy it from them. The top guy in charge of the men in suits looked at me without an ounce of compassion and simply said, "What's it worth to you?"

"$50,000," I said.

"No," he responded.

"Then I'm not buying it, so you'll just have to kill me," I said stone-faced.

"Joey, Joey, Joey, we're businessmen. We're not going to kill you."

I came prepared with the shop's ledger. I opened it up, and we went over it, bill after bill.

"I paid everything," I insisted, leaning into the table and looking them all in the eyes. "I don't owe you anything."

"You're going to risk everything? Not talking to your family," one of them asked.

"I'm not paying you," I said calmly.

I didn't have any reason not to believe they weren't going to kill me or hurt me. It's not like the men in suits were shooting up people in the kitchen, and I never heard a conversation about dropping dead bodies in the river.

I was shaking. I was hurt. I was close with the owners, and they cared for me. And there I was, in front of men in suits, and my friends, the owners, were silent, not standing up for me. I got up and left. My friend watched my back and walked out behind me. On the way out, I looked at my brother-in-law and gave him a head nod. He loved me, and I didn't want to put him in an uncomfortable situation with his family, but there wasn't any way I would even know how to buy something for that amount of money.

Before the topic came up, the idea of owning my own pizzeria never crossed my mind. But after that meeting, it was all I could think about.

One afternoon, I was talking to a friend of mine who knew what happened with the men in suits and my former employer. He told me of a restaurant for sale about a mile down the road from the old shop.

Go check it out," he said to me.

Something clicked inside me during that conversation.

Maybe I could do it.

Not long after I hung up with my friend, I found myself driving back to the pizzeria, and I saw the "For Sale" sign in the restaurant window exactly where he said it'd be. I slammed on the brakes, pulled over to the side, and ran up to the window. I pressed my face up to the glass, shielding the sunlight so I could see as much as possible.

It didn't matter what condition it was in. I was going to buy it. My mind was made up as I was running up to the window. I wanted to show everyone I could build a pizzeria from the ground up.

I called the number on the sign.

"Hello," a woman said when she picked up.

"Hi, I'm calling about the restaurant you have for sale," I said enthusiastically.

"John," she shouted, "this man on the phone is calling about the restaurant."

There was some commotion on the other end of the line, and I heard a man and woman talking in Italian as the phone passed from one person to the other.

"Ah, hello?" The man said with a thick accent, clearing his throat loudly in the earpiece. I leaned away from the phone for a second and introduced myself to him.

"Are you the owner?" I asked.

"My wife and I own it, yes," he said.

I guessed he was older, probably in his late 60s or 70s, just by how he spoke. "What do you want for it?"

"Well, we're asking $100,000 for it with $50,000 down," he said, coughing in between every other word.

I was only 24 years old at the time. I was moving so fast and on pure adrenaline that I didn't stop, slow down, and do the research necessary to know what I was getting into.

I didn't bother asking for a sales report or about the condition of the place. I didn't ask what came with the purchase and what they were keeping. I never thought of getting it inspected first or looking into an alternative avenue for another restaurant.

John explained that he and his wife were ready to retire, and they wanted to buy an R.V. and travel. They seemed like a kind, honest couple, and I thought buyers had been lining up to buy their place, so I moved fast. I didn't even bother asking why the promissory note of the loan was to be paid back to them and not a bank. I assumed everyone who sold a restaurant themselves did business that way.

I knew I'd need to get a loan to help me pay for it. I

figured I could find an investor for some of the money and bet I could get $50,000 in credit, but I wouldn't be able to get the total $100,000 without help.

I jumped off the call with the owner, thinking I had just found a lottery ticket, and immediately dialed my mom's number.

My mom was never excited about me working full time at the pizzeria in the first place, but I was hopeful she could support me with a loan to get my own pizzeria.

In my conversation with my mom, I asked if she could loan me $50,000. "I don't have that to lend you, Joe," she said.

"What about the house?"

"Let me think about how to do that. I could refinance to get you $50,000," she said.

I secured $10,000 from an investor. My mom was able to refinance and lend me $50,000, which I agreed to repay over the course of 15 years. The owners agreed to let me make a payment plan for the remaining $50,000. Once my mom had her refinance wrapped up, I gathered the cash, drove over to the owner's home, and put $50,000 down on their kitchen table. They had paperwork all drawn up for me, including a promissory note with a payment schedule. I agreed to monthly payments of $400, paid directly to the previous owners.

The pressure to pay my mom back was a tight ball in the middle of my gut. The stakes of my success sat like a ton of bricks on my shoulders. And the thought of my mom losing her house because of me left a metallic taste in my mouth.

As soon as I got the keys, I raced straight over to what was about to be called *Carlucci's*. Proudly. My heart was pounding so hard I could hear it echoing in my ear. I blasted my music, beating the steering wheel, excited out of my mind.

I pulled into the parking lot and almost forgot to put my car in park before jumping out of it and running up to the door. My cheek muscles hurt from smiling so hard as I unlocked the door and stepped inside for the first time. I exhaled as I walked around the kitchen and took in what was now mine.

It didn't take long for my bubble to bust and panic set in. I never imagined the deal I made was a bad one. But as I examined the equipment, reality hit me harder and harder with every second.

The pizza oven, the mixer, the stove, and even the refrigerator were all outdated, and a few of them were even broken. Some equipment worked, and I could use it, but eventually, I would need to update everything.

I walked out to the dining room and saw broken furniture that looked twenty or even thirty years old. The wood was rotten, and I didn't want to sit down out of fear that the chair would give out from underneath me.

I was going to have to replace everything out front as well. It was too late to give the place back. It was mine. I looked at my phone and wanted so badly to call up that older couple and cuss them out. But I knew nothing would change the outcome. They screwed me.

Fuck them. I'm not paying them a dime back.

In my mind, I listed out what I needed right away to be able to open the doors and start making my money to pay off the debt to my mom and my investor.

- I needed to clean the place.
- I needed to scrub out the equipment.
- I needed to paint the interior.
- I needed to hire help.
- I needed to get a liquor license, which I knew nothing about.
- I needed ingredients, which would take some time.
- I needed to replace the broken furniture.
- I needed a sign.
- I needed to make menus.
- I needed to buy plates, utensils, glassware, pizza utensils, and serving dishes.

I didn't just buy a money pit and put myself in deep debt. I willingly put myself on the most significant learning curve of my life, yet unknowingly. It never crossed my mind that I would encounter new obstacles, new tasks I knew nothing about, and have only myself to accomplish them.

I was on my own, running out of pure spite.

I fantasized about walking in, dusting everything off, turning on the lights, getting Carlucci's painted on the front door, and bolting to the building in big, bold letters within days. I had been making an ingredient list and running the numbers over and over in my head to make sure I wasn't overextending myself, but I was prepared for the crowd. I imagined that as soon as people knew I was back in business, they'd walk in for a pizza within a few weeks.

That wasn't going to happen.

I decided to take on the liquor license first. That took time. While I waited for that to come back, I looked for cheap but nice-looking furniture. I found new chairs that would take several weeks to come in, and I'd have to assemble them. Before that delivery, I scrubbed out all the equipment by hand, washed everything in the place from the top to the bottom, and then finally asked a bunch of friends to come over and help me paint the interior. Once all of that was finished, I put the menu together and printed it up.

The longer it took me to get the doors open, the further away my dream became. I wasn't making any money during those months, so whatever I had left from my loan was what I used to live on: pay my rent, pay utilities, and feed myself. A silver lining in my life at the time was the fact that I lived with two other people, so my expenses were meager.

It was hard not to slip into a depression during that phase of life. And a glimmer of hope came one afternoon when Dave, who I learned was actually referred to as Big *Dave* in the industry and for obvious reasons, called to check in on me.

It had been months since we had spoken, and it was really good to hear from him. I caught him up to speed about the men in suits, taking a brain break at the carnival, which he gave me hell about, and my new place.

He was excited about Carlucci's and wanted to talk more about New York-style pizza. He was from the Midwest and knew nothing about New York style. He was interested in hearing all about the menu and my recipes, in detail. He wanted to know the measurements and timing. I wasn't worried about him stealing them. He was a genuine guy; I knew that in my bones.

Despite the fact that the first story I heard of his had to do with stealing credit card receipts out of the trash of another pizza place, I knew he was a straight-shooter like me. But I was curious.

"What's with all the questions about New York style?" I laughed.

He told me that he was often hired by restaurants as a consultant, but couldn't ever offer them support on how to make my style of pizza.

"I'm best at New York and Sicilian style pies, so that's what I'll have at Carlucci's," I said.

"Would you ever want to come out on the road with me?" he asked.

"Ah, hell yeah, man. That would be awesome!" I said enthusiastically.

"It'd be for a day or two at a time, and you'd get some good money out of it."

"Sign me up! When do we start?" I laughed.

"I'll call you as soon as I get the next one."

It felt great to have a guy like that on my side. Talking to him was comforting in ways. He had that way about him. He believed in me and cheered me on, even when I had no idea what I was doing.

A few days after my call with Big Dave, I bit the bullet and accepted that I needed help. I was close to opening and still had to hire help and train them on the menu.

I reached out to people I knew in town who might want to join me in my new place. Gratefully, I got two yes responses right away. I needed more than that, though. I put a Help Wanted sign out front and hired a few part-time employees who I felt could hold their own in the kitchen.

By the time everything got delivered, printed, painted,

put away, and I got the staff up-to-speed on the menu, it was November. Months had passed. I wasn't surprised when I got a call from the previous owner's daughter.

"Joe, you have missed the last three payments," she said sternly.

"And I'll continue to miss them. Your parents were dishonest and screwed me. You can tell them to go straight to hell. They aren't getting a fucking dime more out of me," I shouted and hung up.

I was greatly disappointed in the deal and felt betrayed by the kind, nice couple I bought the place from. I'm just a straight-shooter, and I would have never thought of pulling the wool over someone's eyes the way they did to me. I would have told a potential buyer to come in and see the work that had to be done before we made an agreement.

I didn't have a single ounce of remorse for speaking to her the way I did. I hoped she called back so I could do it again.

By mid-November, we were finally ready to open the doors to the public. I told family and friends, hung a banner out front, and kept the front door open during the day, hoping the smell of pizza would bring in some foot traffic. It wasn't extraordinary or extravagant, but it felt great to finally have the place in a condition where I felt proud to welcome people inside.

Making those first few pizzas in Carlucci's was special. I made sure to let each order imprint itself onto my cells, so I'd remember that accomplishment for the rest of my life. As I tossed and stretched dough, laid down sauce, cheese, pepperoni, peppers, sausage, and onion, I thought to myself:

I did this.

It's all happening.

I had so much help and support behind me, helping me make this a reality. I know what I'm doing.

I'm good at this.

This is where I belong.

I took on a massive undertaking, and it is paying off.

I was proud of myself. During those first few days that we were open to the public, I gave myself the benefit of the doubt that more customers would find Carlucci's, and the financial burden chained to my neck would eventually lighten.

And then one day, two men did. They weren't the men I wanted in Carlucci's. I recognized them immediately.

"What the fuck do you want? I asked the men in suits.

They didn't respond. They slowly sat down at a booth and watched me. They took up a table in my place for hours. I called my brother-in-law. He didn't pick up. I called his brother, the owner, and got nowhere there either. Finally, I called my friend who had my back at the last meeting.

"Hey man, can you come over here? Those guys are back?" I said when he picked up.

"Be right there."

He walked in the front door in a tight-fitting T-shirt, so his chest looked puffed up and his biceps showed. He glared at the men in suits as he passed by them. They didn't flinch. They eyed him the whole time as he strolled through the pizzeria into the kitchen, where I was standing.

"What do they want?" he asked me.

"I'm assuming money. They haven't said anything, and they've been here for hours."

I didn't get the feeling that they were going to kill me, but they weren't leaving without money. That much I knew.

"What do you want to do?" my friend asked me.

I assumed they were concealing guns. And we'd be dead within seconds if we tried to jump them. I had a safe hidden in the far back corner of the kitchen, behind bags of flour. I opened it, grabbed my checkbook, wrote a check for two thousand dollars, and walked out to the dining room with my friend on my heels. I slammed the check down in front of them.

"This is all you're getting from me. Now get the fuck out of my shop and do not come back here." I said calmly, loudly, confidently.

Without saying a word to me, one grabbed the check, stuck it in his inside pocket, and they both got up to leave.

As soon as they left, I called a friend who was a lawyer and knew who these men in suits were and what they were all about. I explained everything and was convinced to stop payment on the check right then.

"These fucking guys," he said. "They're bullies. Hang up with me and call the bank right now," he said.

"Seriously?"

"Call me back after you're done."

I knew I was pouring gasoline on the fire by stopping payment, but he seemed to know what he was talking about, and I trusted him. I called the bank, put in a stop payment request, and called my friend back.

"Now look, Joey. You might hear from them again this week. If you do, call me and I'll take care of it."

"Yeah, I'm betting on hearing from them. They are going

to be pissed. I just did that. They better not kill me for this," I laughed, but was pretty serious.

"They aren't going to do that. They want money. They don't want you dead."

Three days later, I got a call at Carlucci's. The men in suits were screaming mad. I was actually surprised it took them that long to call.

"I told you I'm not paying you. I don't owe you a fucking dime. Don't send your goons to my place again. We are finished." I slammed the phone down on the receiver.

I waited no longer than a few seconds before calling my friend, the attorney. "Hey man, they called again."

"Give me a number."

I rattled off the digits.

"I assure you, you'll never hear from them again after today. I will take care of them. You do not have to worry about this anymore."

I believed him. He knew people. And I assumed he had something good on the men in suits. I never heard from them again. And that was fine by me. I was grateful for the training and the lessons. But mainly for the idea that I could own a pizza shop.

Unfortunately, opening a pizzeria that I personally owned was very different than just running one for which someone else was financially responsible. In addition to making sure the staff was doing their jobs, keeping the kitchen clean and tidy, ensuring we were producing the best possible product we could, and keeping everyone paid on time, it was my responsibility to always be searching for new ways to bring in traffic. That one was the most important one of all. Without customers, nothing else mattered. Before I went home that night, I looked for the next time I could try out for the US Pizza Team.

I had been so invested in the shop in Danbury, and keeping my head above water during the summer, and with the time and money sunk into Carlucci's, I had missed two tryouts. The next time I could compete was back in Ohio in January. I had just gotten through the rest of November and December.

I signed myself up for the same competitions as last time and dedicated any free time I had to practicing. I practiced tricks I saw other guys do at the competition, like getting down on the ground while spinning the dough around my legs and rolling the dough from the tips of my fingertips down my arm, behind my neck, and down my other arm. I even had staff members time me as I folded boxes as fast as possible and stretched dough as big as I could without it ripping.

Come January, it was time to head to Ohio again. This time it was just me in the car. But just like last time, after I closed Carlucci's on a Saturday, I drove straight through the night, hopped up on energy drinks. I pulled into the parking lot of the conference center again right before the competition started.

The rules were that once a competitor made the team, they were only allowed to stay on it for a year. The ultimate competitions were held in Italy, and after Italy, any team member had to try out all over again. It seemed like a senseless rule to me, but I was grateful to have another shot at making Tony's team.

It felt rejuvenating to be back in the energy of pizza

competitors. I was around guys who lived to make the US Pizza Team.

I called Big Dave as soon as I checked in and got a chance to meet up with him again before my acrobatic heat. He didn't waste much time telling me about his newest consulting gigs and promising me he was looking for a way to incorporate me into his consulting business.

Big Dave and I ran into Tony as he was in between judging heats. He gave me a pep talk, and I tried my best to listen to him, but my nerves got the best of me. I didn't come in last place in my competitions, but I didn't place either. I wasn't as disappointed as I was the first time. I left Ohio feeling like a million bucks.

It was in New York, at the US Pizza Team Trials event, where Tony and I met a guy about my age named Siler Chapman. He was from South Carolina, always had a smile on his face, and was the nicest, most generous man. But he sucked at acrobatic tossing.

Tony had arranged for CNN to come to the Javits Center to watch and film the acrobatic pizza tossing competition for the US Pizza Team Trials.

The pizza competition scene was starting to catch on and gain attention, as well as fans. Tony was, of course, a hundred steps ahead of everyone else and knew it was just a matter of time before television stations made celebrities out of chefs.

Before the freestyle competition started, the reporter came over to Tony to thank him for inviting her to check out the show. She was looking forward to watching everyone compete, and just then, Siler jumped up on stage, proclaiming he was going to impress her with his tossing skills.

We had never seen him compete before. I could tell Tony was a little nervous, especially with the reporter standing next to him.

Siler's music started. It was a popular rap song at the time, which surprised me because, from the little I knew about him, I learned he was a Christian guy who led ministries. I didn't expect him to toss dough to a song that had a bunch of curse words.

It took Tony seconds to start shifting his weight. He looked uncomfortable. Tense. Worried even. He folded his arms tightly over his chest. His fists were clenched, and I assumed his teeth were too.

Siler was awful. He absolutely bombed. If I hadn't been so concerned with how freaked out Tony looked, I would have felt sorry for Siler. Maybe even asked him how he felt his performance went, because he wasn't remotely close to where Tony set the bar for me or anyone else I knew.

The reporter leaned into Tony and whispered something in her ear. His face went blank, and I heard him assure her that *his guys* would be worth her time. She looked pissed. She was a big deal at the station and had people she had to answer to as well.

Siler got down off the stage. People sort of clapped, but not nearly enough for my comfort level. Tony looked at me and said, "You better be a hell of a lot better than that."

"I got this," I said, nodding my head and heading to the stage.

I felt confident, and I loved the crowd. I thrived off of it.

The more, the better. And knowing there was a cameraman and a reporter in the audience fueled me.

I loved every second of the competition. And I was good at it. I tossed pizza dough around my waist, through my legs, over my shoulders, and got down on the ground and kept the pizza going. It was thrilling. And to do it in front of a crowd, as well as Tony again, just fed my ego a healthy dose.

It was amazing. I killed it. The crowd loved it, and when I finished, I saw Tony smiling from ear to ear, applauding in a way that felt like we won something that wasn't just mine but his, too.

Everything with CNN went the way Tony envisioned, but I didn't make the team. Not surprisingly, neither did Siler. I was disappointed but knew I would get back on eventually. The way the team was set up every year made it possible for me to try out in a few months in Los Angeles.

I found a spot to chill, out of the way, while CNN interviewed Tony. I admired how natural he looked in front of the camera and how professional he conducted himself. I was like a wild stallion compared to him. I knew I had the drive and motivation, but my method was much more chaotic than his.

After that was finished, I watched him hand Siler his plastic pizza dough discs and tell him to go home and practice. He'd need a lot of practice if he wanted to make the team Tony put together.

Not long after, my next competition started. This time it was for the largest stretch. I knew Tony was going to be my judge again. And this time, I was determined to listen to him.

We made eye contact before my heat, and he gave me a little nod before he counted down the clock. I took that to mean, *don't fuck up again, hothead.*

So, I didn't. I was excited that I didn't rip the dough the way I did years prior, but I didn't win first place. I got second. I was still pretty proud of myself for placing second. The people I competed against were veterans, clearly competing for years. I had limited experience in the world of pizza competitions.

Tony was encouraging and told me to keep at it. He didn't want me to get discouraged since I had one more event to compete in before the end of the day. My last competition was my strongest event—the fasting pizza-making competition. We had to take a 10-ounce dough ball, stretch it, slap it, and place it on a 12-inch pizza screen. Acrobatics was semi-new to me, competing and making a competition team was definitely new to me. But making pizza dough as fast as I could was something I could do with my eyes closed.

I walked out to my spot and looked down at the dough. Before I knew what really happened, the whole thing was over. I missed first place by seconds. I looked up to see Tony's face. He looked confused. I watched Tony talk to a few of the judges and was shocked when he came up to me and told me I was heading to Italy. The pizza maker who came in first place also placed first in a different contest. The rule was that the same pizza maker could not compete in more than one event.

Adrenaline rushed through my body, and it was hard to contain my excitement. I had no idea what it meant to travel across the world and compete in a pizza-making contest against Italians who were probably fed pizza before they had teeth, but I was pumped. I wanted to prove myself to the natives, the doubters, and probably even myself.

I made the US Pizza Team and, most importantly, redeemed myself in front of Tony, for whom I already had tremendous respect and admiration.

I was overflowing with pride, and grateful I was heading to Italy.

CHAPTER THREE

MAKING THE TEAM

After making the team, Tony took me under his wing. He became more like a brother to me—a mentor, really.

Four months went by before we competed in Italy. And during that time, Tony called me to ask how business was going and if I needed anything. I appreciated his concern for me, but I wasn't ready to admit how badly I was struggling. The truth was, I needed help. I was barely getting by financially, always working, exhausted, and couldn't see a way out. But I could not say that to Tony.

"Things are great, man," I'd always say. With excitement, I was hoping that saying it out loud would eventually make it true.

Finally, I got a call from the US Pizza Team about my trip to Italy. I gave her my information, preferred time to fly out, and schedule. Later that day, I got an email with my ticket confirmation. It made the whole thing real. For the first time in my life, I was leaving the country. And the fact that I was on a United States competition team, traveling to the birthplace of pizza, made the experience that much more special. I felt important, validated, and even grown up. I double checked the time and date and felt a bubble of excitement wash over me.

I printed my ticket, told my staff when I'd be away, and sent Tony a text message.

Got my ticket. See you in New York.

The next month, I made sure I ordered everything Carlucci's could possibly need while I was in Italy. I got to the airport in plenty of time and found Tony and his wife waiting for me inside the terminal. The US Pizza Team made sure we were all traveling together. We had a few hours to kill before our flight to Italy.

Maybe it was the sleep deprivation or how easy it was to talk to Tony, or how supportive his wife was to both of us, but while waiting for our flight, I finally shared how badly Carlucci's was coming along and how underwater I felt.

"I think I need to close Carlucci's," I told Tony.

"I'm sorry to hear that," Tony said.

We went on to dissect issues, pitfalls, and even solutions, but ultimately, there was very little that could be done other than gain access to a wheelbarrow of cash to pay off the bank note.

"Let's see if the trip does anything for it," Tony said, smiling.

I nodded and appreciated his encouragement. When I boarded the plane, I told myself I was going to enjoy everything Italy had to offer me and make it a memorable trip, in case I never came back.

Going to Italy with Tony felt a little bit like returning to the motherland with the Godfather himself. It was old hat for him, so I just watched what he did, went where he went, and repeated what he said. He had set up a few meetings before the competition started. One of them was with a flour company called Caputo. He asked me if I wanted to go with him to meet the representatives. I jumped at the chance to have direct relationships with an Italian flour vendor.

The day after we arrived, Tony and I met two well-dressed men in suits in the lobby of our hotel. These men in suits were not like Rocco, Luca, or Giovanni. They were polished and sophisticated. One spoke broken English, and neither of us spoke Italian, so Tony grabbed a guy to translate for us.

The intention of the meeting was to get Tony to do a seminar/demonstration with a Caputo representative at the pizza expo. And Tony wanted these guys to know he meant business. Through the translator, we were told to follow the men in suits to their car. It didn't take long for us to arrive at the boat docks. Tony and I looked at each other and had the same reaction.

Fuck. What are we doing at the docks?

I mentally prepared myself to fight off two men who I assumed brought us out there to kill us for some fucked up reason. I didn't know what Tony was thinking, but I didn't fly around the world to get wacked by men in suits. I clenched my fists as I got out of the car.

"What did you get us into, asshole?" I whispered to Tony.

"You go first," he said.

We put some distance between us and the Italians and slowly followed them down to a boat. The guy who spoke a little English jumped on board and pulled out two boxes for us.

We weren't expecting anything from these guys, but instead of killing us, they actually gave us watches.

"Gift," he said.

"Jesus," I sighed. "They're giving us watches?"

"Holy shit," Tony whispered.

"I thought they were going to kill us," I laughed.

"You and me both."

Tony and I climbed onto the boat and thanked them for our watches. We took seats at the front of the boat and enjoyed a peaceful ride around. Neither of us knew why we were on a boat or why they gave us watches. We didn't have an interpreter and never talked business.

We got back to the hotel in time for dinner with Tony's wife and the rest of the US Pizza Team. We told everyone about the misunderstanding of assuming we were getting whacked on a boat by the mob. I keep my affiliation with men in suits back in New York to myself.

As far as my competition went, I knew I was good. But I also knew I wasn't good enough to bring home prize money yet, so I made a game plan for myself.

Since I was already on a team making waves and going against the grain, I figured I would take it one step further in my solo competition. To make myself stand out, as an American competing in Italy, I decided to make a pizza in the shape of Italy. It ruffled feathers, got a lot of attention, and as a result, I made a name for myself.

I didn't place in Italy in my solo competition, but the news of competing brought on a bunch of media attention back home, and Carlucci's was packed for months. The press alleviated some financial pressure I was facing, but not enough to get out of the mounting debt I faced. But I relished in it. And when the time came to compete again in Los Angeles a few months later,

I registered for all the individual competitions again.

- Fastest Pizza
- Largest Dough
- Acrobatic
- Fastest Pizza Box Folding
- Best Pizza

A few weeks later, it was time to close up Carlucci's and hop on a red eye across the country, bound for the City of Angeles. I tried to sleep on the plane, but I was too excited. I sat with my eyes closed, listening to 50 Cent, blink-182, The White Stripes, Toby Keith, and visualized myself competing. I went through every event, one by one, and pictured myself walking up onto the platform, getting ready, and moving fast, accurately, and with ease.

In my visualization, I won everything. Maybe that calmed my nerves or psyched me up enough to go into the 2003 trials in Los Angeles a bit differently, but I was noticeably in a different frame of mind when we landed.

I grabbed a rental car and headed out across town to the convention center. I checked in and wandered around for a while, looking for Tony and Big Dave, but instead bumped into Siler. I was surprised to see him since he bombed in New York.

He was always smiling and looked like he had just rolled out of bed. Considering I just got off a plane and hadn't showered yet, I assumed I looked the same.

We walked around for a bit and then sat our stuff down and started practicing tossing plastic discs around. He was better than the last time I saw him. But I knew I was better too.

While I was warming up for my Acrobatic, I thought back to the plane ride out to Los Angeles. I closed my eyes again and found my way down onto the floor, tossing the practice dough around my legs and up into the air, catching it without any trouble. It gave me an idea. I was always looking for that one thing to put me in a different light or give me a slight advantage or some additional buzz than my competitors.

I should do it blindfolded.

I finished practicing and looked around for a napkin or someone wearing a tie I could use to wrap around my eyes. I found a red, white, and blue bandana for sale at one of the pop-up stores at the convention. I folded it in half, tied it around my face to make sure it was going to work. It fit perfectly. After I paid for it, I kept it folded in my back pocket.

I didn't tell anyone what I had planned to do. When my name was called to compete in acrobatics, I walked out to the center of the stage with the bandana around my neck. Before I started, I lifted it up over my eyes, and the crowd went nuts. I felt a surge of excitement run through my body, and I performed perfectly. I knew when I finished there wasn't any way I could come in second. I knew I won.

But Siler did really well. And that shocked the hell out

of both Tony and me. And he tied with me for first, so we both made the team and were both heading to Italy on the US Pizza Team.

A magazine interviewed me before I caught my flight back home about why I decided to do the competition blindfolded and if I planned to do that again in Italy. I laughed it off, knowing there wasn't a chance in hell I was going to place in Italy. Those guys were masters and practiced tossing dough around like it was their full-time job. I was just lucky to be an American going back to compete against the best of the best.

The competition in Italy didn't happen for eight months after I tied for first in Los Angeles. I had plenty of time to practice. And Tony made sure I practiced. Whenever I competed and did well, the press found out about it, and business at Carlucci's increased for a while. I needed it. Things were different though after California. Mainstream national media representatives called me.

A few days after I got back to my normal life, I got a call from an unknown number with a 310 area code. I knew it was a Los Angeles number, but wasn't expecting it to be an associate producer from *The Ellen DeGeneres Show*.

I hit *accept* and speaker phone. "Hello," I said.

"Hi, is this Joe?"

"Yeah, who's this?"

She introduced herself and told me she heard about my blindfolded routine in Los Angeles the weekend before.

"Okay," I laughed.

I was busy getting the kitchen prepped for our dinner rush, so I was really only half listening to what she was saying.

She asked me questions about my life and how I got into the pizza business, about Carlucci's, my time in Italy, and why I decided to compete with a bandana around my face.

I had no idea where the conversation was leading or why she really called. When she wrapped up the call I thanked her for her time and went back to my ingredients.

Tony called almost immediately after I hung up the phone. *Jesus. I need to prepare for dinner. Can't I get a minute here?*

"What's up?" I said.

"Hey, I gave a producer at the Ellen show your number," Tony said.

"She just called."

"How'd it go?" Tony asked.

"I don't know. Okay, I guess."

"Did you sound like a dick like you do right now?"

"What," I laughed.

"That was an interview. If you didn't show up like you would on TV, all excited and pumped up like you're a kid high on candy, you didn't get it."

"Oh, I didn't know that."

"Yeah, you probably blew that," Tony sneered.

"Jesus, how was I supposed to know?" I shouted.

"I'm sending another producer your way."

"With who?"

"ESPN. Don't fuck it up," Tony said and hung up the phone.

Don't fuck it up. It echoed in my mind. He was always saying that to me.

I went back to work and wasn't surprised when I got another call from an unknown number within the hour.

This time, I answered the phone like it was my favorite person on the planet and gave the producer my full attention. I walked outside to get away from my staff. I paced around behind Carlucci's, literally jumping up and down, going through every detail of the competition in Los Angeles I could think of, and I got booked on a show called *Cold Pizza*, which ESPN aired.

Got it. I texted Tony.

Good. Siler got Ellen.

That stung for a second. But I brushed it off as quickly as I could and walked back into Carlucci's like nothing happened, which wasn't too far off from the truth. Just because I got booked on a national television show didn't mean anything until it aired. And all I was told was that someone would be in touch with me to confirm details about the show.

Life went on like normal. Well, somewhat normal. After *Cold Pizza* aired on ESPN later that month, business did pick up some. And I got another call from Tony.

This time, he congratulated me on the television appearance and told me he wanted us to go to Italy to compete as a team, much like the Europeans did. It sounded great in theory, but considering we lived all over the country, we couldn't practice as a team like the Italians or the Germans.

"Let's meet in Ohio in two weeks," he said.

"Okay, see you then."

I contemplated driving there to avoid the cost of the flight, but in the end booked an early morning flight and slept on the plane. I got to the hotel to meet the guys a little before everyone else. I took the extra time to check in with Big Dave and some friends I hadn't spoken to in a while.

When we were all together, Tony handed each of us a script. The idea he had in his head was that the five of us were going to do synchronized pizza tossing.

He wanted something no other team had. Most other pizza competition teams had one or two great guys who would stand in the front and perform all the hard tricks, and the rest of the team members would just stand in the back like shmucks and try not to fuck up.

We weren't going to look or be like that. Tony said he wanted to create something that was a combination of figure skating and Harlem globetrotting. We were going to have costumes, and the performances would have storylines.

Every member of the team was important, and each of us had a different script to remember. It felt great to belong to a group going somewhere. Tony was so focused and so much further along in his career than me. And I knew we were onto something really big.

He told us our first performance was going to be to the Matrix, and my script looked like this:

> Walk to the stage behind Siler. Give each other four feet.
>
> When Tony counts 1-2-3, turn to face the audience.
>
> Once the music starts, wait three counts, then slowly lower to a crouching stance on the ground.

Single-hand spin with right, take a step to the right.

Single-hand spin with left, take a step to the left. Small toss with the left, take a step to the left.

Small toss with the right, take a step to the right. Turn to face Siler.

Behind-the-back catch.

Behind-the-back catch. Behind-the-back catch. Behind-the-back catch.

Turn to face the audience. Flip and roll.

Flip and roll.

Over the head. Under the right leg. Under the left leg.

Body wrap. Body wrap.

Turn to face Michael.

Toss the pizza to Michael. Catch pizza from Michael. Repeat three times.

Walk eight counts to the right, doing one-handed spins as Tony goes in the center.

Over-the-shoulder catch. Over-the-shoulder catch.

High toss and spin. High toss and spin.

Turn inward toward the center of the circle.

Walk toward the center of the circle toward Tony.

Toss in front with the right hand, lift the left knee.
Toss in front with left hand, lift right knee.

Behind the back catch. Sky high.

Toss the pizza to Tony.

Rolling down the shoulders from right to left,
then left to right. Sky High.

Get down on the ground.

Under the right leg. Under the left leg. Under the
right leg. Under the left leg.

Sky High. Stand up. Take sunglasses off. Bow.

Walk off stage.

As I read the script, I thought, *What the fuck? This is crazy.*

I'd experienced a lot of craziness by that point in my life. People thought working two jobs, buying a pizzeria, hell, even competing in a pizza tossing event, was crazy. I liked crazy. It worked for me. I looked around at everyone else's faces. The guys were laughing and giddy like little kids who just got their first win on a video game. They were lit up, excited to go against the grain, do something that wasn't done before, and make some waves. It was pretty obvious everyone was on board, and I knew we were about to have a wild time together.

One by one, we looked at Tony, waiting for him to say something.

"This is going to be a lot of work," he said, his hands on his hips, chest puffed up. "You're going to work like a dog and practice till you drop. We are going to be fucking perfect at this and we're going to win."

He was our leader, and I followed him to the best of my ability. But being in my mid-20s and struggling with financial problems, a failing restaurant, and having undiagnosed ADHD, following wasn't something that came easily or without complaints. Ultimately, I had the utmost respect for him and what he saw for me and my life. And I knew the others felt the same way.

We all nodded. Agreeing. Ready to work. Having no idea what we were getting ourselves into.

We worked like dogs that weekend in Ohio. Tony kept us in a hotel room, and we practiced around the clock for two days. We each had a different script. He compared it to a movie script. Everyone had different *lines* to learn. And once we came together, prepared with our own individual script, it would make sense and fit. I'd be going one way, Michael would be going the other way, and then suddenly, we're all circling each other, tossing together and in sync. It was brilliant. If one of us screwed up, dropped the dough, or was too fast or too slow, Tony would stop the routine and make us start over.

We were as strong as the weakest link and practice made perfection. And we practiced while we were dripping with sweat. Just like Tony said we would.

When we weren't practicing, the guys and I were still getting to know one another. Siler and I became fast friends. More like brothers, really. Tony had us room together. We were each other's opposites. I was fast-paced, ready to go at a moment's notice, and had trouble calming down, and Siler was cool and uber-chill to the point where he wouldn't get out of bed unless I grabbed the mattress and yanked it out from underneath him. I was the loud New Yorker, and he was the Southern charmer. Yin and Yang. He sort of fell into the pizza industry like me, but much later than I did. Siler was all set to become a mechanical engineer and had a change of heart after September 11th, 2001.

After we all went our separate ways, we had a month at home where we had to practice our script by ourselves. Tony would call, email or text if he couldn't get a hold of me.

Are you practicing? How's it going?

What part are you struggling with? Are you doing it to music?

I knew him well enough that he wouldn't leave me alone if I dodged him, so I was honest and up front. He was relentless with the stirring of our ship. He was focused and on a mission to kick ass in Italy.

Yes, I'm practicing when I have time. It's fine.

I'm not struggling. I got it. No, I'm not doing it to music.

I knew he wanted me to practice to music, but I was practicing in between everything else I had to do to keep Carlucci's afloat, not the other way around. When I saw his name and number on my phone, I figured he was calling to bitch me out.

"Hey man," I said.

"Pack your bags, Joe!" he shouted over the phone. "We're heading to Munich first!"

"Germany? What for?" I yelled back.

"A grocery store over there is asking us for a demonstration of our routine. It'd be great practice before the competition in Italy," he said.

"Wait a minute, then. Are we flying into Germany and then flying into Italy?"

"We'll take a train into Italy."

"Jesus," I sighed.

It sounded like a ton of coordination and mentally draining. While I was grateful I wasn't the one driving the bus and getting all the guys to and from various countries, it was a lot to prepare for. But I did as I was told.

I packed for Germany and Italy. I was never into fashion or anything fancy. I made sure I had clean jeans, a lot of shorts because knowing Tony we were going to practice a ton. I grabbed a bunch of T-shirts and one nice button down just in case we went somewhere I needed to look like a business owner and not a pizza tosser. I packed my plastic dough discs and chef's jacket.

A few weeks later, I was locked in a hotel room with Tony, Siler, Ken, and Michael, practicing our routine eighteen hours a day and sweating like pigs. It was grueling and exhausting. I'd never seen a sweat lodge before, but I believe Tony created one for us in that hotel. It smelled like the wrestling room of my old high school.

We never stopped. In the middle of the night, after practicing for eighteen hours, Tony suggested we take a break. Siler and I wanted to go downstairs to our room and crash for an hour. Tony wasn't having that. We both got showers in, collapsed on top of our beds for a few minutes, but knew if we fell asleep, Tony would go ballistic.

I jumped out of bed, ready to go. *One speed—Attack!* My body ached. I moaned a bit and stretched my arms above my head.

"Hey, get up!" I shouted at Siler. He didn't move.

"Siler!" I yelled louder.

I was worried Tony would kick him off the team if he got back upstairs. I grabbed a little coffee cup from the wet bar, filled it with water, and splashed his face as I hollered as loud as possible, "Wake up! We gotta get back."

"I'm up," he said breathlessly.

Siler moved as fast as he could, which wasn't all that quick. I laughed as he stumbled a few feet from his bed to the bathroom. He splashed water on his face, put his shoes back on, and we were back in Tony's room within our allotted break time.

We practiced for several more hours before I noticed the sun was rising. I could see it peeking through the curtains.

"Let's take a break and get something to eat and check in with our staff and families," Tony said.

Siler and I grabbed coffee and a light breakfast in the lobby of the hotel while the others went back to their rooms to crash.

We finished our eggs and coffee, grabbed our plastic dough discs from the floor where we dropped them, and went back upstairs to Tony's room.

We both sighed as we waited for Tony to answer. I was preparing for another long day, similar to the day before.

Except now we had the added pressure of having to perform the following day for the first time as a team. Ken and Michael were already there waiting for us to begin practice.

Tony turned on the music as soon as Siler and I got into position. By now, it was our second day of practice, and we were going on no sleep. It wasn't just my body that was exhausted. I was starting to get tired mentally.

Practice went on and on that day. Tony gave us additional breaks throughout the day, and then finally, come sunset, we were told to get dinner and a good night's sleep. But when it was time for me to close my eyes and fall asleep, all I could do was mentally repeat the routine over and over in my head. I looked over at Siler's bed and saw he was wide awake as well.

I felt ready. My nerves were pretty steady. I remembered every step I had to do, what toss I had to make, and when I had to make it. The rest of the guys were doing pretty well, too. It was just a matter of time. We were a young team that only had a handful of days together a year.

Tony, even then, was a phenomenal tosser. His speed was unlike any of ours. He had to slow his throws down to match ours. Siler was slow, and Tony was always on his back to speed up. Michael and I were somewhere in the middle.

We weren't scheduled to practice at the crack of dawn. We had to pack up our stuff, check-out, get over to the grocery store with enough time to practice a few times in the space they had set up for us.

Tony didn't just agree for us to do one demonstration in Germany. We had three shows lined up on the same day. And once our last demo was done, we had to race over to the train station to catch a ride and start making our way to Italy.

We looked at the shows in Germany as a warm up for Italy. We made sure we looked sharp and as identical as possible. A crowd showed up for us at every hour we were scheduled to perform. They loved it. We did good the first time, better the second, and even better the last time.

It was a long day. The shows were scheduled within ninety minutes of one another. Everyone was bone tired, stressed that our businesses were all experiencing some sort of crisis, and to top it all off, the payment Tony thought was going to happen for us, didn't.

We watched money exchange hands in front of us. The man who recruited us to come to Germany gave a wad of cash to someone associated with the US Pizza Team, and none of it ever came to us.

We did it all for free. We were pissed, felt taken advantage of, and ready to get the hell out of Germany.

After that last show, we grabbed our bags and headed straight to the train station. It wouldn't have been bad if we had a flight from Germany to Italy. But heading south on the train was a nearly twenty hour ride. We had to catch three different trains and had some waiting time between each leg.

By the time we got to Italy and got to the airport to pick up the rest of the US Pizza Team for the competition, the guys and I had been up for nearly two days straight. We were at each other's throats.

I told Tony to go fuck himself at least twice. And I threatened to quit a few times, too. The entire experience was disappointing. The last thing I wanted to do was compete in a foreign country.

I was ready to go home. Actually, we all were.

To make matters even worse, we totally bombed the acrobatic tossing competition in Italy. We came in dead last. We were embarrassed. All that hard work, sweat lodge experience, and Tony's dream for us went to shit. Ultimately, we needed more time and more time to practice.

Joe and I go back decades. To see him successful now after all he's been through is really sweet. I know it hasn't come easily to him. It would have been an easier road for him if he could have put his ego and arrogance aside and just listened to me. But sometimes that was the hardest thing for him. He had so much growing up to do. He had so much to learn about himself, his pride, and how to trust people. And he always chose to do it the hard way. When we first met, he was cocky and got in his own way. He was unfocused and would make simple mistakes and blow them out of proportion. His nerves seemed to get the best of him on more than one occasion, although he'd never admit that. He wanted everyone to think he was hardcore or had skin as thick as steel. Nothing could get to him. But being as close as we all were back then, traveling the world together, stuck in a room for 18 hours a day, practicing as a team, I got to know him personally, and he's just like everyone else. He wanted to make something great out of his life. And to get to the top, he had to learn from his mistakes.

I remember this one time I took Joe and the team to the Pittsburgh Food Show. It was 2006. I wanted them to try Neapolitan pizza. I told them it was going to be the next big thing, and they should all bring it to their restaurants. Joe practically spit it out on the table and talked shit about it in front of the chef. Five years later, he asked me for a recipe. Twenty years later, he's making it.

He's learned how to let that chip on his shoulder go and step back from being the loudest person in the room to learning how to lead and listen. I'm proud of him and what he's done for himself and his staff. It's been a long time coming.

Tony Gemignani

CHAPTER FOUR

THE MARSHAL

COMING BACK FROM ITALY THAT SECOND TIME WAS like a dream. Press was everywhere. People asked for my autograph and to stop and take a photo with them. It was amazing and overwhelming. I didn't know how to sustain it.

From the outside looking in, it probably seemed like I was rolling in cash and everything was turning up aces. But the reality was, I wasn't close to being out of debt, and I still hadn't paid a single dime back on the promissory note. I couldn't get over how betrayed I felt by the previous owners and how embarrassed I was by not knowing what to ask before I bought the place.

One afternoon, I got a visit from the marshals. I was given a notice that stated I had to pay the full amount of the loan back in thirty days or I was going to lose the place. And that was it. I wasn't paying the note to the previous owners. I figured I was running on thin ice as it was, but I was lost on what to do to gain that much cash in a month. So, I just kept going, with my head down, working as hard as I could.

I wasn't ready to give up Carlucci's without one last

battle. I couldn't just let it go. Every day for the next month, I looked for additional loans, new competitions to enter to try to win some quick cash, but came up empty-handed.

The last day of the month came. I treated it like a normal day, the best I could. We were open for business. I told the staff what was happening and my closest customers that it was our last day. That night, I cried as I watched the marshal close the doors to Carlucci's and padlock the place.

The marshal knew Carlucci's. He loved it and was really sad to do his job that day. He apologized for being the one to close the doors on me, but I didn't let him leave without setting him right.

"I put my blood, sweat, and tears into Carlucci's. It just wasn't enough, and it's nobody else's fault but my own," I said.

We shook hands and went our separate ways.

I knew I had to break the news to my mom, but I wasn't ready to just yet.

I gave myself the night to feel the disappointment and shame for having a padlock on the front doors of my pizzeria, and the overwhelming sensation of not knowing where to go next. People who knew me in town and had my number called me all night, asking me what was happening.

Was I okay? Did I need help?

I wasn't ready to admit the truth, so I let calls go to voicemail.

I wasn't ok. But I didn't want their help either. I didn't know what I was going to do next, but I didn't want to ask for help or share my story with people who used to pay me to make dinner for them. I got a little sleep that night.

Before the rest of the world woke up, I hit the gym to get rid of some pent-up energy. I avoided eye contact and kept my head down, earbuds in and music loud. I went hard and fast.

I was angry, upset, and frustrated, and with every set I did, it felt like I was reliving the last handful of years all over again.

I saw Rocco, Luca, and Giovanni flash through my head. I saw the competitions, Tony, Big Dave, the praise, Italy, and finally the marshal. It was like a nightmare I just couldn't wake up from. On the ride home from the gym, I knew I had to call my mom. I waited until I was back at home, took a deep breath, and called her.

I let out a long exhale while I waited for her to pick up.

"Good morning, Joe," she said when she picked up.

It was early in the morning, and I could tell she was just getting her day going. "Mom, I have to tell you something," I said.

"Oh no, what happened?"

"The marshals came yesterday and locked up the shop."

"I know how hard you work. I'm fine. I know you'll pay it back."

That was it. She gave me such grace in a situation she didn't have to. I hated having to make that call. She was understanding. I was going to pay her back what I owed her. That wasn't changing. And she knew that just because she knew me. But before I hung up the phone with her, I said it out loud so it was clear. To her. To me. And to God. Come hell or high water, I was getting her that money.

"I'll figure something out, Mom."

"I know, Joe. I'm not worried," she said again.

I felt a massive boulder move off my chest, and for the first time in a while, I could breathe deeper.

I hung up with my mom and got some breakfast together. While I ate I put a plan on paper.

I was going to tell Tony and Big Dave to put some feelers out into the local community, to say that I was looking for a job and to look into filing for bankruptcy.

My next call was to Big Dave. I don't know what I was expecting from him. Maybe some direction on what to do next, or perhaps news that he had a consulting gig I could jump on right away. But instead, he gave me a two-line pep talk.

"It's a bump in the road. Brush yourself off and get back up on the horse," he said.

"Yeah. You're right," I said.

I wasn't someone who stayed down long. I didn't have the choice in this case. I had a huge debt to pay back, and the longer I sat in a self-destructive state of mind, the worse off I'd be. But before I could do anything else, I had to tell Tony.

"I'm sorry, Joe," he said sympathetically.

Hearing the concern in his voice made my throat tighten. I didn't hear shame or guilt or disappointment. I knew he was my friend and wanted the best for me. That touched me.

"Let me fly you out here for a long weekend. It'll do you good to clear your head in the California sunshine. You can stay busy or lay low, whatever you want," he said.

I tried to protest but he didn't let me get too far down that road before insisting I come out for a visit. And truthfully, I needed a break. Not only for my mind but my body too. I was burned out and exhausted.

That next weekend, I got on a flight early Friday morning and was in California mid-day. Tony drove me right to his pizzeria and I jumped into the kitchen alongside him and worked wherever I could the next few days. It was good, and busier than any other pizzeria I had ever worked in. I was encouraged and inspired. And even though I flew across the country to work in another pizzeria, it was different.

By the end of the weekend, Tony offered me a job in his pizzeria. He cared about me and felt so terrible for what I was going through. But my ego wouldn't or couldn't accept his generosity or help. It felt like the easy way out of a hole in the ground. Something was preventing me from letting myself off the hook. I needed to prove to everyone that I wasn't a failure in that business. What mattered was that I was a world-class pizza champion, down on my luck, and I wanted to find my way to the top. On my own.

I thanked Tony but told him I had to do this on my own. He understood. I got back from California, not knowing if I'd feel any different from when I left. Depression was present, but didn't have a death grip on me.

That Monday morning, I went back to my action item list. The last thing I had to do was file for bankruptcy. I searched online and found an attorney in Danbury, Connecticut not far from where I lived. My mom's boyfriend at the time offered to attend the meeting with me since I never did anything like that before.

"Just one more life lesson Carlucci's taught me," I laughed as I called up the attorney and made an appointment for later in the week.

I was told the meeting was $500 up front and to come

prepared with a list of creditors I owed money to. My mom's boyfriend and I arrived with plenty of time. I had my checkbook in one hand and a short list of vendors in the other. It felt good to have a parent figure there with me.

We sat down and immediately got down to business. There wasn't a lot of talk or emotion involved, which I was grateful for. Not having to go into the backend story or behind-the-scenes details about what had led me to sit in front of the attorney was refreshing. He was professional, courteous, and quick.

The act of filing for bankruptcy wasn't as big as the idea. I wondered about what people were thinking or saying about me. But sitting there in that office, it was as easy as buying an appliance, but as much paperwork as buying a car.

List out creditors here.

Sign here, there, and initial at the bottom of every page. Leave without the worry and concern of creditors calling.

And in my case, I left the meeting with a fresh outlook. I knew the pizza business. I could run pizzerias. I could get a job at another shop if I wanted to. The feelers I put out before I went out to visit Tony had come back with some options to help out at a few local places. Nothing felt aligned though.

I thought about going back to work at the hospital for a day but realized that felt too much like taking a step backward. I wanted to leap forward somehow. I realized I needed to try something totally different.

And that's what I did. I wanted to try something that I hadn't done before. And something that would help me bring in the cash so I could pay my mom back.

My mom was working at a telecommunications company

at the time and asked me if I wanted an introduction. Selling phones was something I never saw myself doing. Then again, neither was filing for bankruptcy.

I interviewed for a sales position at a big-name, multi-billion-dollar corporation and got it. "If you're anything like your mom, you'll do great here."

Getting the job offer fueled the fire in my belly. I hung up my apron, put on a suit and tie, and ran at the opportunity at full speed. I didn't slow down. I knew I had to get to work and move on with my life to the best of my ability.

I'm a workaholic by nature, and in a position where I could make as much as possible by selling something I didn't have to make with my own two hands or buy with money in my own bank account felt exhilarating.

I worked all seven days from 8:00 a.m. to 4:00 p.m. and quickly rose to the top sales position in the Tri-State area. And it showed. I was getting showered with gifts.

- Floor seats at the Knicks.
- Vacations
- Prizes

It would have been so easy to be happy in a sales position. And if I wanted to travel, impress a lady with floor seats to a professional game, or drive a luxury car, I could have. I never dreamt of being a guy with six figures in the bank, but that was the path I was on. And I was young enough where if I kept going, I could make truckloads of money, pay off the loan even earlier, be clear of debt, and could even look at retirement savings and buying my own home. Hell, maybe even two. All I had to do was keep my head down and run. No other sales representative could touch me when it came to the results.

The loan was $400 a month, and I'd make my monthly payments and sometimes throw more money at it each month.

I had a good enough life with friends all around me. Every day was different. I could have had whatever I wanted. But the entrepreneur spirit that was lit on fire a few years prior was dead weight inside. There was this heaviness, like grief, I couldn't shake but could feel. It was like a part of me was broken. There was a massive void in my life. I could see it in my eyes when I looked at myself in the mirror. It wasn't from just one person either. It was from the previous few years, and getting kicked in the teeth over and over again.

One night, on the drive home, I was stopped at a red light and noticed a Help Wanted sign in the window of a pizzeria. I knew the place. They had decent pizza. I liked the owner. And without hesitation, I pulled around the corner, parked the car, and walked in. I said hello to the staff and asked if the manager was around. To my surprise, he came out and knew who I was. He told me I was overqualified to be a part-time pizza maker, but I didn't care. It wasn't about the money or the position. Being in the environment again did something for my spirit that selling telecommunications to big billion-dollar companies didn't.

"I'll take whatever you have and can start working right now if you need," I said.

"Alright, if you're ok with a later shift and turning pizzas out, I'd be happy to have you," he said.

We shook hands, and I started the next night.

I was so excited to get through my shift the following day. When I clocked out at 3:00 p.m., I hit the gym quickly and then rushed over to the pizzeria to start at 4:00 p.m. I was ready, willing, and looking forward to getting back into the kitchen, the industry, and the energy of a pizzeria. It was like I hadn't skipped a beat either. The muscle memory was there, my hands knew what to do, and my whole body felt alive as I turned out product for the next six hours. Before I knew it, my shift was over, and it was time to head home.

I got in my car, turned on the ignition, and just sat there for a few minutes. I felt different. I was happy and felt fulfilled after a long day. I didn't feel exhausted or worried. I loved the pizza business. I loved the kitchen, the relationships in the business. I missed the fast-paced energy and environment of it all. I craved the noise and the excitement of what would happen each day. The joy the pizza business brought to me wasn't anywhere close to what I felt selling phones.

I couldn't wait to get back inside the pizzeria and do it all over again.

For months on end, my day consisted of a 7:00 a.m. – 3:00 p.m. shift at the telecommunications store and a 4:00 p.m. – 10:00 p.m. shift at the pizzeria. It wasn't the first or even second time in my life that I was holding down two jobs.

Despite how busy my life was, I could feel the passion and joy in my spirit again. After a while, the excitement wore off, and it turned into my normal everyday routine, and I loved it. That is, until I'd see an unknown number pop up on my phone.

I wanted to be able to fully move on with my life, but couldn't. I'd be reminded of my failure all the time because of the constant calls from debt collectors. They started calling not long after I filed for bankruptcy and never let up.

I assumed I'd get a letter in the mail letting me know my paperwork for bankruptcy was accepted and the debt was cleared. I'd check my mailbox every day, looking for one, but it never came.

When I filed for bankruptcy, I was told the debt collector calls would stop, since it's against the law for a collection agency to hassle someone in bankruptcy.

One afternoon, during my lunch hour from the telecommunications shift, I grabbed a newspaper to kill time and recognized a face. It was a mugshot. The article was about the attorney who helped me file for bankruptcy. He had just been arrested for fraud and was dying of cancer in prison.

My mind went into a full panic mode. I called my mom, her boyfriend, Tony and Big Dave, and with all my conversations pieced together I landed on the assumption that I was taken care of, and everything was going to be alright. There wasn't anything else I could do and so I just kept moving on.

While talking to Tony, he reminded me that I could come out to California and work for him. I just couldn't accept it. I felt so ashamed of what had unfolded in my life, and it felt like my mess to fix.

The bag of debt instantly felt like a rope around my neck. It wasn't against the law for collection agencies to call me. I owed the bank $100,000.

Between paying back my mom and the bank, I was looking at years of paying everyone off. I felt like I was making a dent in my payments with my mom, but once the bag of debt from the bank came rushing back into my life, there was no way I could speed up my pace to sell anything faster.

I finished my day, sold some products, and took a drive before heading to the pizzeria. I wanted to clear my head before my next shift. I couldn't change what happened or go back and do anything differently. What I could control was how I spent my time and my attitude each day.

It wasn't long after realizing I had been duped that the owner of the pizzeria came to me one night after my shift and offered me a full-time position. The shop was busier than ever, and he needed me in the kitchen more than I could manage as a part-time employee. And he could see I felt more aligned standing there in a pizza kitchen than I did in a suit and tie selling telecommunication products to him as a business owner. I took it without hesitation or a second thought.

It felt so right in every cell of my body. The second I accepted the offer, I felt lighter. The void in my heart shrunk and the rope around my neck loosened. The debt was still there, but I was going to pay it back on my terms, doing something I loved to do.

As soon as I put my notice in with the billion dollar big boys, I got three different calls. First from the district manager, then from the regional manager, finally from the vice president. They all asked me if I knew what I was doing. And all three of them asked me what more I needed from them in order to stay and continue bringing in big bags of money for them.

"I appreciate what you're saying," I said. "But my heart is not in your company. I've made up my mind."

"You're our top salesperson in the New England area, and you're leaving a great, steady sales job for a pizza job in Danbury, Connecticut?" the vice president asked.

"Yes, sir. I am."

Leaving the steady sales job felt freeing, not risky. The more time that passed, the more I realized clocking in and out of that sales job was more like a death sentence than an opportunity for a better life. Anyone could do that job. All it took was tenacity. There were a million people hungry just like me who would have loved to step right into my footprint and do even better than I.

I wanted to do something with my life that nobody else could do. I needed my contribution in life to be uniquely mine. Being around Big Dave, Michael, and Tony changed the way I saw my future.

I didn't just want to clock in and make someone else a shit ton of money. I wanted to create a life I was proud of on my terms, like Siler. And be wildly successful, so I could lift others up like Tony.

What was I created to do? What was my purpose? What felt right for me?

Working behind the counter at someone else's pizzeria wasn't the end-all-be-all job. I knew that. But for the time being, it was a step in the right direction, and it felt more aligned than anywhere else.

I worked hard. I kept my head down. And I loved it. I had a rhythm and everyone around me conformed to my pace, my beat.

After I got my feet underneath me, I let Big Dave and Tony know where I landed.

"Perfect timing," Tony said.

"Why's that?" I laughed.

"The Italian Festival is happening in Virginia Beach, and I need you there for a demo."

"Easy. Done."

"The other guys are coming too. I have something I need to talk to you all about."

He was being secretive and protective. He didn't need to say anything else to me though. I would have come without any other agenda beyond him telling me I needed to be somewhere.

I called Siler as soon as I hung up with Tony. He and I coordinated our flights so we both got into Norfolk at the same time. I bought an airline ticket, requested time off from the pizzeria, and looked forward to seeing my friends again.

Later that week, Tony sent out instructions to meet him in his hotel room the night before the competition at 6:00 p.m.

Siler and I gave ourselves enough time to work that morning, fly into town in the afternoon, catch up about our lives, and grab something small to eat before our secret meeting with Tony.

We agreed to meet up at a restaurant bar. I saw him approaching from down the hallway. I could see him smiling, ear-to-ear.

"Hey, man," he said cheerfully, as he always does.

It was good to see him again. I was grateful I didn't have to rehash the hardship of losing Carlucci's or getting swindled by that asshole attorney who never filed bankruptcy on my behalf. It was under the rug. Old news. From the second we greeted each other, we started messing around. He looked like he hadn't shaved in days. I looked like I hadn't slept in days. Both were probably true. We jabbed at one another about still being single and shared thoughts about what Tony wanted to discuss.

We found our way over to the hotel, dropped off our stuff, ran across the street to get a sandwich, and knocked on Tony's door a few minutes early. Ken and Michael were already there.

"The gang's all here," Tony said, welcoming us into his room. I hugged everyone, thrilled to be around the guys again.

I could feel the part of me that died with Carlucci's starting to wake up. We stood there, staring at Tony. He told us to sit down.

"Jesus," I whispered, expecting to hear the news that someone had died or that he was getting bought out for billions.

"Listen. I have an idea for a team. I worked it all out. We can be independent operators, get sponsored, and do it our way. And if we do this right, we won't have to compete or throw another pizza, ever," Tony said.

His eyes were huge. He was steady. Almost whispering, like he was worried a spy was in the ceiling or something.

"I want to teach you what the Pizza Expo was like in the 90s. We will bring back the World Pizza Games to the Las Vegas convention. I want us to be on the cover of Pizza Today magazine. We're going to really shake things up."

We all gawked at him like he was speaking French.

"What are you talking about?" I laughed.

"I want us to be pioneers in changing the pizza industry," he said wide-eyed and smiling from ear-to-ear.

Siler and I exchanged looks that said something along the lines of, *yeah... he's definitely on something.*

"This is what I want us to do, together as a unified team," Tony said, so excited he was practically jumping around the room. "I want us to go to the Javits Center to compete in the US Pizza Team Trials—as a team called the World Pizza Champions. I want us to dress in a uniform that means business. I want us to meet with trade publications—as a team."

"And say what," I laughed.

"That we're bringing back the World Pizza Games to the International Pizza Expo next year."

He put his hands on his hips and looked us all in the eyes one by one. We stayed quiet for a minute and then, as if we planned it, all of us, Siler, Michael, Ken, me and Tony started yelling, clapping, hopping around the room like crazy teenagers who just won the state championship.

The energy in the room was unlike anything I'd experienced yet. We just agreed to change our lives. There was a fork in the road, and we all turned left, with Tony guiding us like he knew the way. Again. Seeing something nobody else could see. And thanks to Tony, I've had a lot of life-altering moments already.

Later that night, Tony took us to a well-known pizzeria in town that was doing something unique. At least, unique for the time. His friend was making wood-fired Neapolitan pizzas.

"It's what's happening next," Tony said.

We all laughed. I thought it tasted like shit.

But Tony always knew what was happening before the rest of us.

CHAPTER FIVE

FAMOUS JOE'S

A FEW MONTHS LATER, IT WAS TIME TO MEET TONY and the guys at the Javits Center in New York City. It didn't take me longer than a few hours to get to the convention center. I got on the road before the sunrise and stopped to fill up on gas and grab a coffee. I didn't get stuck in too much traffic and pulled into the hotel shortly before we were all scheduled to meet with the editors of *Pizza Today.*

I parked my car and texted Tony.

I'm here. Where are you at? Conference room.

I didn't bother checking into my room. I figured I could do that after our meeting with the magazine. The sooner I met up with the guys, the better. I grabbed my duffle bag from the back seat and made my way upstairs. I saw Siler not too far ahead of me as I rode the escalator up to the conference floor. I called out for him to wait for me, and we walked into the room together.

Tony looked anxious. Hell, I was anxious. We were about to announce the fact that we were creating a disturbance in the pizza force field. Anything could happen. There were a lot of *what-ifs* in the air.

The president and vice president of *Pizza Today* arrived right on time. We all introduced ourselves and sat down at a long conference table, them on one side and us on the other. Tony didn't wait long to announce that we were forming the World Pizza Champions at the US Pizza Team Trials and wanted to bring back the World Pizza Games at the next expo, which was put on and sponsored by *Pizza Today.*

"We'll do everything," Tony said to the editors, who looked at him the same way we did the last time we heard it.

He went on to say, "You just need to pay for our airfare and hotel accommodations, and we'll take care of the rest."

Tony had a way about him. It was hard to argue with him. After he explained that we'd turn down any placement any of us would receive in the US Pizza Team Trials competition we were there for, he shared that we already had sponsorship to compete in Italy as the World Pizza Champions. And when asked why we were forming an entirely different team and concept, we all chimed in.

"To promote and help the mom-and-pop shops across the country."

There were more mom-and-pop pizza places around the United States than big chains. And someone needed to support the underdog. Like me. And most of us.

We walked out of the conference room as World Pizza Champions, with an agreement that *Pizza Today* would not only let us all host, organize, and judge the World Pizza Games in Las Vegas during the next Pizza Expo, but they'd pay our way to do it.

Step one done.

It felt like a huge relief to have that meeting over with. If I felt a burden off my back, I couldn't imagine how Tony felt. I'd glance at him from time to time to get a reading, but he was cool, calm, and collected.

As soon as the president and vice president walked out of the room, I expected some downtime to unpack the meeting, but we had just enough time to change into the uniforms Tony ordered for us.

It was surreal. I felt a buzzing run through my body as soon as I held it up in front of me.

It looked like a race car driver's suit. It was a black jumpsuit with sponsor logos all over the place and in big red letters—WORLD PIZZA CHAMPIONS. I smiled and looked around at the guys. They all had smiles plastered on their faces, too. The room was quiet as we changed, but I could feel the weight of the moment.

For someone outside the industry, what we were doing could have seemed silly or unimportant. But here we were, declaring ourselves champions and coming together to lift each other up and stick together as a team. The World Pizza Champions team. From a competitive perspective, the pizza competition wasn't like the Olympics, where only so many people from the same country could compete. Anyone could start a team. It's just that nobody had done it before us.

We marched into the US Pizza Team Trials in a single row, one after another, in our new uniforms. We walked fast and didn't stop to talk to anyone. People turned to look at us, pointed at us, and talked about us. The buzz started even before we stepped foot inside the convention center.

We each competed in every event, even Tony. He hadn't competed in years. He wasn't allowed to, but as the new captain of the World Pizza Champions, he could.

We were all the best we'd ever been. The excitement, attention, and momentum from the news surrounded us. It fed me. Then again, I always enjoyed the audience. We wanted to make a splash, and we did. People swarmed us, asking about the rumors of World Pizza Champions, and our meeting with *Pizza Today* had just happened.

Not everyone was as excited about the way we handled the announcement, though. Despite the fact that we all competed at a level of pure excellence, our scores were dog shit. Even Tony's. I came in last place. I didn't think that was at all fairly earned or justified. Tony came in first place but got screwed over. We watched the judges change their scores to knock him down to second place.

At that point, I had kept my cool for a long time. I'd lost two pizzerias by that point, been threatened by the men in suits, and owed a shit-ton of money to a couple who didn't deserve my hard earned cash. But witnessing my friend being mistreated was something I just couldn't stand for. It was the straw that broke my back.

"That's bullshit!" I shouted when Tony's scores changed.

He tried to calm me down, but I was far past that. I got in the face of a judge and shared my concern for their ethics. I used words like deceitful and underhanded. It didn't take long for things to escalate and State Troopers to show up. I was so close to the judge's face that I could feel him breathing on me. And that's when I was escorted out of the convention. Tony and the rest of the guys followed me out.

If we walked in together as the World Pizza Champions, we were leaving together, too.

After the Javits Center, we went back to our respected cities and Tony sent us moves to practice and music to practice to. We had a massive disadvantage compared to other teams. Most other teams were pizza makers in the same town, maybe the same region. Our team was made up of Tony and Ken, in California, me in Connecticut, Siler in North Carolina, and Michael in Ohio.

Other teams had daily practices and years of friendship; if not friendship, they at least knew each other well enough to know their quirks and tempers. We had to pick a weekend that everyone was free, fly somewhere to meet up and learn a routine quickly, and then we were on our own to practice until the competitions. We were like the Monkeys. We were all cast and then thrown into the circus of performing pretty quickly afterward.

We blew up and became celebrities in our own right in the industry. We kept our word and relaunched World Pizza Games in the United States at the next Pizza Expo. We organized it and I judged the fastest dough slinger, fastest box maker, largest stretch, and acrobats. It felt great to be in a position to support my peers. The World Pizza Games went off smoothly, and that didn't shock anyone. We all knew it would be with Tony at the helm. They were exhausting, though, and from Las Vegas, we jumped on a plane to compete in Italy as the World Pizza Champions.

Our first routine as World Pizza Champions was to the Matrix. Even though we had competed with it before, it felt different as World Pizza Champions. Our routine was very dramatic and different from anything else any other team did. We even dressed up like actors from the movie with long black coats instead of chefs' jackets, our hair slicked back and black sunglasses on. Tony played the antagonist, and the rest of us circled him, tossing pizza dough back and forth to him, as if they were ninja stars or bullets.

The routine was great. Entertaining. Memorable. And it should have been. We worked like dogs for that performance. Per usual, we arrived a few days before the competition and locked ourselves in a hotel room for 18 hours, sweating like pigs and practicing until our muscles ached and we had blisters on our fingers.

But it was worth it. Typically synchronized routines highlighted one person. That wasn't what World Pizza Champions was about. We all played a role. And we had to get used to the rhythm of everyone else on the team.

We were all really impressed with our first time out as World Pizza Champions. We placed second, losing by one point.

I came back to Connecticut and stepped right back into my day job as the main pizza guy at the pizzeria I worked for. But this time, customers knew me, asked for me, and wanted my autograph and picture. It was uncomfortable but exciting. The more we competed, the better we got, and the more attention the World Pizza Champions received.

It didn't take long for more pizzaiolos to want to join the World Pizza Champions, and Food Network to call. They put us on the first-ever Food Network Pizza Challenge, competing against each other. It was Tony, Silver, Michael, and me. We were filmed in Cleveland, Ohio. It wasn't far to travel for me, which was great.

The Food Network fans loved it. Which brought the producers of the *Food Network Pizza Challenge* back to us shortly after the show aired. We were invited to compete again, this time at the Mall of America in Minnesota. The network positioned the segment as world-champion pizza acrobats battling it out for a Guinness World Record.

We had three categories to compete in:

1. Highest pizza toss
2. Best tasting
3. Largest stretch

We had ten minutes to put a gourmet pizza together using 10 ingredients, and whoever won received $10,000.

We all wanted it, of course, and for different reasons. The title would have been cool, but the cash and recognition were something I really wanted. Being able to split $10,000 between my mom and the bank would have been the biggest win for me. Tony ended up winning the best tasting, and I was happy for him.

I won the title for the highest toss. Tony won the title for the largest stretch, but only by a quarter of an inch.

Since we organized the World Pizza Games, we couldn't ever compete in them so for the next several years, my time was divided into judging the World Pizza Games at Pizza Expos and traveling the world to compete as a World Pizza Champion.

The guys and I went to Turkey, Germany, the Dominican Republic, and all over the United States. We made a ton of money, which I appreciated. Tony choreographed two other routines for us—one to *Star Wars* and the other one to *The Godfather*.

One year, while judging the World Pizza Games at the Javits Center in New York City, I met a successful restaurateur who was there competing. He did alright in his competitions, but nothing out of the ordinary.

After judging his fastest pizza heat, he came up to me to introduce himself. As it turned out, Bob and I were from the same city. I didn't know him, but he knew me. I was impressed with him. He was a smooth talker, and based on the success of his seven restaurants, I figured he knew what he was doing in the industry. We exchanged numbers and agreed to meet up for lunch when we got back home. He went his way, and I went mine, and I figured it was just one of those encounters that nothing more would come from.

Some time went on, and I forgot about Bob.

The more I traveled and competed with World Pizza Champions, the stronger the itch to be my own boss again became. Just as Carlucci's came out of the blue, one night while driving down the street, I noticed a pizzeria I loved had a *temporarily closed* sign on the door.

I felt a rush hit my chest, and heat instantly rose to my face. I knew the feeling. Something sparked inside, and I couldn't wait to get home and research why that place, which typically had a line around the block, was closed.

It didn't take me long to see the owners had legal issues. And it didn't take long to find out who the landlord was and to get a sit down meeting with him a few days later in an office building not far from the pizzeria.

I dressed in street clothes and walked in with the mindset

that I was just acquiring information, not signing anything or making any rash decisions. But when the landlord told me the rent was only $900 a month, I had a hard time not jumping out of my chair screaming, *I'll take it.*

I kept my cool, shook his hand, and thanked him for his time. As I was walking out, a man dressed nicer than I stopped me to tell me he recognized who I was, loved Carlucci's, and wanted to help me get the money together to buy the place. It was hard to see the chain of events as anything other than God-sent.

As I was preparing to go down the road to give owning a pizzeria a second attempt, I got a call from Bob, the well-known restaurateur I met at the Javits Center.

"Hey man," I said when I picked up the call. Bob laughed and said, "Joe, what's going on?"

We had a little small talk, nothing too important. But the more we talked, the more I realized he was someone I could actually benefit from learning from since he owned so many restaurants. So, I decided to tell him I was looking at buying another shop.

"Oh yeah? Whereabouts?" He asked.

I told him the address and gave him details about the location, and what I knew about the current owners and landlord.

"Yeah, man, that sounds like it could be a great opportunity for you. Your name is well known here, and you've got a following. I'm sure it'd be successful," Bob said.

"I don't know about all that, but I appreciate you saying it," I laughed.

He suggested we get together for lunch that week at one

of his places. I agreed. I knew he was looking at getting more involved in the competition scene. I assumed he wanted to talk about World Pizza Champions, Italy, maybe the Food Network. I had never been to any of his restaurants before, so I was eager to see the menu, how it operated and his role in the business.

Lunch was relaxing. The food was great. The conversation was easy. We shot the shit and talked about the industry, and he treated me as if I'm his equal. I appreciated it, even though I knew we weren't equals. He had seven restaurants to his name, and from the outside looking in, he was a huge success. We weren't even in the same arena in terms of ownership experience, but that day, I was grateful to hear we had the same types of troubles and were always looking for new ways to bring in business.

We exchanged ideas like I do with Tony or any of the other guys I've traveled the world with. I expected him to ask me more about the competition scene and joining World Pizza Champions, but instead, he offered to come look at the place I wanted to buy with me. I was thrilled to get some insight into my next possible venture from a guy who knew more about owning and operating restaurants than I did.

We took his car to the shop and looked in the windows. I ran through what I'd change and what I envisioned for the place. He was impressed.

"Let me show you my places now," Bob said after we got done looking over the space I wanted to buy.

I went along with it. I didn't have anything to do for another few hours and figured it wouldn't hurt to see his concepts. He drove me to each and every one of his restaurants and then invited me over to his million-dollar home, where his very sexy, seductive niece happened to be waiting for us. And in front of her, he said he was interested in buying the space.

I looked at him, pretty shocked, and took a few seconds to think about what to say. "Now, let me explain," he said quickly.

"Great. Please do," I said.

"I want to buy that little 900-square-foot place, make it a pizzeria, and have you be the face of it."

"'Be the face of it'?"

"Yeah. We'll be partners," he said, smiling.

I glanced from his niece back to him and couldn't help but smile back. "What do you mean by 'be the face of it'?"

"You're the boss of the local pizza scene," he said. "Why wouldn't you be the face of it?"

All I saw were stars. This guy had weight, I believed he knew what he was doing, and I trusted him. His niece didn't hurt either.

"Alright, let's do it," I said. "Fantastic," he shouted.

We shook hands and he said we'd work out the details later. He drove me back to my car in one of his other vehicles. On the front floorboard was a Famous Ray's bag. I picked it up and crumpled it up in my hands, holding it so he'd remember to throw it out.

"Let's call the new place, Famous Joe's," he said.

I looked at him, assuming he was kidding. "No way, I'm not comfortable with that."

"Joe. You'll be famous one day. It's called Famous Joe's."

That was it. Before we got back to my car, the place was named. My head was spinning. The day took a sharp turn, and I had no idea what was up or what was down. I tried not to think too much more about what unfolded. I drove straight to work and did my job without telling anyone anything about my day. But my muscle memory kicked in and I could do my job without really thinking too hard. My mind would wander, and moments from the day would flash before my eyes while I stretched dough out.

So many questions popped into my head.

Did I really want to get back into business with someone?

I don't know much about this guy.

Famous Joe's would be amazing. Is this really it for me?

That night, I looked around the kitchen and took it all in. I was so grateful for the steady job. I loved it. It served me well. I wasn't the owner though. It wasn't my name on the door, on the menu's, or the take-home boxes. I was just a guy trying to find his footing after getting kicked in the gut one too many times.

I thought about the owner and his generosity to me, and my heart ached. He was so kind to me. He let me work hard, keep my head down, and gave me the flexibility to pick up and travel and compete. I hoped he knew I wasn't going to stick around to take over the place for him. We'd never talked about it, and he wasn't anywhere close to retiring. I was grateful for the opportunity to get my feet back in the fire, but it was time to move on.

I didn't know when I'd be moving on, but I knew it would be soon. I didn't say anything to him that night, but let myself feel what it would feel like to be the face of Famous Joe's as I finished my shift.

My new potential partner didn't let grass grow under his

feet. The next day Bob called me and told me his plan. He wanted to rebuild the space for Famous Joe's. He wanted to remodel, upgrade, and even called in a few guys already to start making blueprints to submit. He was on it. I sat and listened to him and nodded along with him. It all sounded like a dream. And really expensive.

I didn't have that kind of cash, and Bob knew it.

"How much do you think that's going to cost?" I asked.

"Oh, don't worry about it. It'll be expensive, absolutely, but it's a must for a concept like Famous Joe's."

"I don't have that amount of money, though, to put in at 50/50," I laughed.

"Let's not worry about that right now. We can figure that out later."

I just went along with it. Bob suggested that I put in my notice at the place I'd been working at so I could work my way through his restaurants while Famous Joe's got remodeled. It sounded like a reasonable plan. I wanted to see how things flowed when he wasn't around. Even though I was excited to start my new venture, I was sad to leave the place.

A week later, I was in the thick of one of Bob's restaurants doing my thing. For the next month, I jumped around from place to place, spending no more than a few days in the same location.

Bob and I didn't talk much, nor did we really ever see each other. I didn't see plans for Famous Joe's, get updated on what was happening with permits or approvals, or even get paid for working in his operation.

About three weeks into my new routine of working for him, six days a week, twelve hours a day, I called him and asked about my payment. We agreed he'd pay me $400 a week while Famous Joe's was getting built out.

"What do you mean, when do you get paid?" Bob asked me.

"I haven't been paid yet, man," I laughed.

He was pretty furious, which I was grateful for because otherwise, I'd be suspicious. "Give me a minute," he said and hung up.

Not long after, he called me with the bookkeeper on the three-way. "Why hasn't Joe been paid?" Bob shouted.

The bookkeeper had no idea why I wasn't paid. He had no idea I wasn't getting paid, and they owed me $1,200 by that point.

"He needs to be paid today," Bob yelled and disconnected the three of us.

I never said a word. But later that day, I was able to pick up my first check. It definitely put me on high-alert. From that point on, until Famous Joe's was built, I called the bookkeeper directly if a week went by and I wasn't paid.

Gratefully, and as if divinely timed, one day during a stressful span of having to wait too long for a paycheck, Big Dave called about a consulting gig I could get in on in Kentucky. And while I was doing a job with Big Dave, a man named Joe Moore came over to learn from Dave. I was always looking for new people and new opportunities to expand my network. I was grateful because Joe and I hit it off. The three of us worked well together, and I impressed Joe with my knowledge of the industry and New York-style pizza. He was opening a restaurant in Alabama and asked me to come down to help him when he opened.

Finally, a year later, Famous Joe's was ready to open.

A few days later, I was sent paperwork for the new place I was to be the front guy and face for. Things really felt like they were coming together for me. When I reviewed the paperwork, I was surprised. I didn't see my name on anything. I wasn't coming on as a partner or owner. The place was going to be named after me, but I wasn't on a single piece of paper.

"Hey, what's this contract, and why isn't my name in it?" I asked him.

"We, we aren't partners yet. You didn't put in any cash up front, so instead of paying you $1,000, we'll pay you $500, and the rest will go toward the loan. And when the loan is paid off, you'll be a partner."

I learned that Bob had bought Famous Joe's with a friend of his, a silent partner I never met. I called both Tony and Big Dave and asked for their opinion.

They both said the same thing to me. "Be careful."

They had concerns about me about getting into business with anyone who wasn't offering a legal contract where we'd be 50/50 partners. I didn't listen to them. I wanted Famous Joe's so bad it hurt. And I felt like I was already in too deep to turn back. I saw red flags. But the desire to be known for my own place was so deep, I ignored it all and the advice from my friends and mentors, and agreed to the path laid out in front of me.

Like every other job I had, I worked like a dog and became obsessed with Famous Joe's. The difference between Famous Joe's and Carlucci's was that I wasn't the owner on paper.

Unfortunately, it didn't take long for things to unwind with Famous Joe's. Like Tony and Big Dave warned me, what appeared to be too good to be real, actually was. Sadly, like Carlucci's there were weeks I wasn't paid, sometimes months.

Bob was a psychopath. He had a bigger temper than I did. I'd seen him cuss out employees, and he even threw a whole pizza pie in my face once. He was a snake. Not long into our venture together at Famous Joe's, I started hearing rumblings about how dirty his business dealings had been in the past, and I regretted putting my name on anything he owned.

Six months into being open, he sold his half of it to his friend named Sam, who had no business in the restaurant industry yet alone the pizza space. He had never owned a pizzeria before in his life and walked in like he knew everything. I couldn't control what he did with his half of the business.

And since the store wasn't doing as well as Sam thought it would, he wasn't making his payments to Bob. When I wasn't paid for weeks on end, things were incredibly stressful. For everyone.

And for the next two years, life goes on, frantically. I was always struggling. I was still competing with World Pizza Champions. I traveled to Italy again. I judged competitions at the World Pizza Games. I was paying back loans when I had some spare cash, but life was challenging. I was able to rent a room from a high school friend, so my overhead was low.

And I was left to carry Famous Joes by myself because Sam had no idea what needed to be done to keep a pizzeria afloat. I checked in with Joe Moore to see how his restaurant was coming along, questioning whether it would ever really open. Joe had always reassured me things were moving forward just at a snail's pace. He was new to the restaurant business and doing it on his own.

The highlight of that time in my life was falling in love with a woman I met while marketing Famous Joe's. We clicked right away and within a matter of months, I moved in with her. She understood my schedule and since Famous Joe's was next to a nightclub and open until 3:00 a.m. Thursday—Saturday, we didn't see each other when other couples got to spend time together.

Finally, in 2008, Joe called with an opportunity for me to come down and help him get the restaurant open. I told Schmuck I was leaving, and he needed to manage Famous Joe's until I got back. I jumped in the car and drove down.

Dave wasn't able to join me, so Tony came with me.

I was gone from Famous Joe's for three weeks. But since I didn't have as much invested in it, and wasn't getting paid like promised, I didn't mind spending three weeks in Alabama with Tony helping Joe Moore open his new place called Tortora's.

Tony and I worked 15 hours a day, and all I did during those days was talk about ingredients and pizza and vendors with Joe, Tony, and Joe's staff. I never bothered checking in with my girlfriend at the time because I was so focused and grateful for the consulting gig.

Plus, I was receiving more money than I'd ever seen in one paycheck for our time. I held it in my hands and looked at the zeros. It felt so great to get paid for my worth. I knew I deserved money like that hand-over-fist for how hard I'd been working for so long. I wanted more. I knew I could earn more.

I was grateful to be acknowledged and saw that paycheck as validation for who I was as a man and my contribution to the world.

As Tony and I worked for Joe Moore, we stayed with Joe's brother-in-law and sister, Julie, and got really close with them. I felt nurtured and supported. It was almost like a bed-and-breakfast. They did my laundry and fed me. And the longer I spent in Alabama, the more comfortable I got and the less stressed I became.

I started to question if going back to Famous Joe's was the right move for me. I knew I had to because my conscience just couldn't get up and quit. But I hated driving back to Connecticut from Alabama. My stomach was in a tight knot the whole drive home. It was 15 hours of pure hell. I knew I was making a mistake going back to Danbury. Every time I stopped for gas, I second-guessed my decision to keep driving. There wasn't anything for me in Danbury. Even the relationship I was in at the time was strained because of my workload.

She and I were living together, barely seeing one another because of my work schedule. We never spoke. We were estranged roommates more than lovers at that point. And it had been that way for months on end. It was over with. I knew it. I'm sure she did too.

I drove right up to Famous Joe's when I pulled into town. It was about 8:00 p.m. We were still open. At least, we were supposed to be, but nobody was there. The lights were off inside. The door was closed and locked. I drove around back to walk through the kitchen and was shocked. It looked like a bomb had gone off inside. Shit was everywhere. Ingredients left out and open. Flour covered every inch of the kitchen. The sink was piled up with crusty cookware. Garbage was spilling over onto the floor.

The knot in my stomach grew into a burn. My throat closed up, and my heart raced.

"What the fuck," I shouted, expecting someone to come out from the back to answer for the mess inside.

That was the sign I needed to leave for good. I shut the door, locked it up, and called Bob and told him I was done. I wasn't coming back.

I drove home. When I got back to my place, my clothes were in a garbage bag out front. I didn't even bother turning off the car. I grabbed the bag, threw it in the back of the car, and crashed at a buddy's house. I stayed in town for a week to attend my nephew's First Communion party at my sister's house. I kept in touch with Korey and Julie, all the while being told Joe Moore wanted me back down in Alabama.

The First Communion party was nice and being around family felt great. But as the night went on, the urge to drive back to Alabama got louder and louder. I knew in my gut it was the right move for me. At dinner, I made my announcement and told my family I was moving to Alabama that night. They all looked at me like I was crazy, but when I said good-bye to everyone, I got back on the highway heading to Alabama.

I drove for hours before stopping at a rest stop for a bit. I caught a few hours of sleep in my car, grabbed some gas station coffee and fueled up. I called Joe's brother-in-law, Korey, on the way down, telling him what happened.

Without hesitation he offered me a room in his house for free and we'd work something out with Joe at Tortora's and I accepted. I said yes to both opportunities.

CHAPTER SIX

ALABAMA

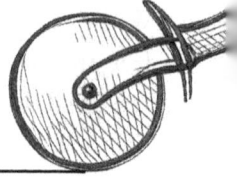

I PULLED INTO KOREY AND JULIE'S HOUSE A LITTLE after 1:00 p.m. the next day. I was exhausted, having been up for more than 24 hours straight. The caffeine I'd pumped into my body to keep me awake on the road wore off as I was approaching Huntsville, and I could barely keep my eyes open. Nobody was home when I got back, which was alright with me. I needed sleep. I walked right into my bedroom, kicked off my shoes, and fell onto the bed. I didn't wake up until I heard some rustling in the kitchen about five hours later.

It took me a few seconds to remember where I was. I pushed myself out of bed and took a minute to get oriented. I took a deep breath and stretched my arms above my head. I did an internal check to see how my body felt after such a shitstorm of a day. I wasn't surprised that the knot in my gut was gone. I knew it would be as soon as I left Danbury, all the bullshit that took place there once and for all. I still couldn't believe I was out of Connecticut. I sat there on the edge of the bed and took a few minutes to reflect on my journey—the road to Alabama.

Men in suits.

Untrustworthy business assholes. Failures.

Heartbreak. Bankruptcy.

It was all gone.

I was on my way to a fresh start. A brand new journey. I'd never imagine myself anywhere but the East Coast. But I felt so grateful to be back at Julie and Korey's. It was the first time since I started working in the pizza industry that I felt at ease. There was peace around me. In me. I knew I had a lot of responsibility in front of me, and I couldn't just live rent-free forever with whatever I owned in a garbage bag in the corner of a spare bedroom. But for the time being, I felt settled. At home.

Julie and Korey were in the kitchen making dinner when I came out. They hugged me and offered me something to eat. We ate together as a family and created a plan for the next few weeks.

We agreed that I'd get in early and prep the kitchen and help with inventory and work six days a week. I'd have one day off but rarely took it. And Tortora's was so chaotic and busy that they welcomed the help and knew I could be flexible on where I worked each day.

For the next several weeks, that's all I did. I called Tony and Big Dave to let them both know what had happened and where I was living. They both knew Joe, Korey, and Julie, and couldn't have been more supportive of me moving down to Alabama.

It wasn't all smooth sailing. No New Yorker automatically fits into the South. And I was a big, fat neon flashing sign everywhere I went. I spoke faster than everyone. I moved faster than everyone. I could get more done and juggle more. But some of that was because of being in the restaurant industry and working like a dog in kitchens. The other part was just me and my pace. I had to move fast, or I didn't know what to do with myself.

There wasn't a blending that naturally occurred for me. I had to learn pretty quickly what Southern sayings meant, and all the different tones the same Southern saying could be said in. I got *Bless Your Heart* in a sarcastic manner and then a sweet one. It took me a while to realize the sweet one wasn't actually all that sweet.

My style, flair, and speed were not always something people appreciated right away, but once they got a chance to talk to me, they warmed up to me.

There wasn't any competition or judging I had to do with World Pizza Champions, so I kept my head down and stayed focused on a rhythm I created for my life. Six days a week, my schedule consisted of working out at a gym I found, running whatever errands Julie and Korey needed me to do, and getting to Tortora's a few hours before opening to prep the kitchen. I worked until the last employee was done cleaning up that night. On Sundays, I rested.

After about a month, Joe and I finally sat down to discuss how I'd fit into the business long-term. He offered me the general manager's position.

"I'll take it," I laughed.

I figured he was going to offer me some sort of salary position, but didn't know what title or how much he'd pay me.

"What do you want for a salary?" he asked me.

That was the first time I was asked to put a number around my time, energy, and worth, and I had no idea what to ask for. I took a minute to look up what managers in the restaurant industry in Alabama were making that year.

"How's $50,000?" I asked.

"Let's do $55,000," he said.

"Thank you, Joe," I said, holding back tears.

"Plus insurance."

Joe trusted me. And for good reason. I had been in his kitchen, helped create his menu, and launched his restaurant. I proved that I could be trusted with his brand and his staff. And because of that, he gave me a lot of freedom. It was essentially mine to run. I didn't own a place like Carlucci's, I wasn't promised a partnership, and then some shady deal like Famous Joe's.

Tortora's was Joe Moore's. I was his general manager. Those lines were clear. But I had a ton of room to hire who I wanted, fire who needed to be let go of, and train those who needed more training.

We shook hands on it, but it felt more like a moment when I should have hugged him. I kept it professional, though. As soon as the conversation was through, I went back into the kitchen, and he moved on to his next topic. I was bursting inside, but I'm sure from the outside I looked as intense as I usually do.

Nothing really changed overnight. Life was going great. I felt good, loved putting roots down in the area, and was grateful for being busier than ever before without the added stress of having it all on my shoulders.

Julie and Korey assured me they weren't in a rush to get

me out of their spare room, so we agreed on a rent price that was reasonable, within my budget, and helped them pay a bill each month.

After about a month, I got a call from my best friend in New York, who was still working at Famous Joe's. I didn't want to hear about the pizzeria. Since I didn't own it, I couldn't do anything about it still being open, but I just never wanted to know how it was doing. I debated about picking up the call for a split second, but he and I went way back and never avoided a call from him before. I wasn't going to start because of a shitty businessman.

I was working when I got the call. We were having a slower night, so I could walk away for a few minutes.

"Hey, what's going on?" I asked as I stepped into the back office.

"You got an envelope here," he said.

"From who?"

"District of Connecticut."

"What?"

"Looks official. Want me to open it?"

"Yeah. Fuck, what's this about now?"

My heart started racing, and my gut balled up into a gigantic knot. I thought I was done with Connecticut.

What more could these fuckers want?

"It's a court order for a payment of $100,000 for Carlucci's," he said.

"What the fuck?"

"I'm sorry, man," he said.

My stomach dropped, and I could have thrown up right on the spot. I didn't understand what happened. I thought when the marshals came and shut down Carlucci's, and I filed for bankruptcy, I didn't owe anything to anyone. Clearly, that asshole I filed with screwed me, stole my money, and never actually filed on my behalf.

Fuck.

"Can you mail that down to me?"

"Of course. It's in the mail tomorrow morning."

We hung up, and I sat there in the office for a few minutes trying to think about what to do next. My throat felt tight. I knew I had to get out of the restaurant because I felt myself start to break down. I didn't want anyone to know my business. I didn't want to make a scene or open up about my past. I took a deep breath, cleared my throat, swallowed hard, and pushed down any tears or look of panic.

I walked out of the back office and casually, as casually as I could, that is, told as many staff members as I saw that I was leaving for a bit to take care of something. Everyone nodded. I walked out the back door without any more hesitation. As soon as I got in the car, I turned the key over and pulled out. I called Julie from the car before I even got my seatbelt on.

She picked up the phone in her usual chipper voice, and I just broke down. I was distraught and spilled my guts to her.

"Just come home," she said worriedly.

I could barely breathe. I couldn't respond. "Drive safe, Joe," she cried.

That snapped me out of my downward spiral. I had people who cared about me. I had to pull it together. I pulled over on the road and took a few deep breaths.

"Okay, I said. I got it. I'm okay."

"Want Korey to come get you?"

"No, I'm almost home."

"Drive slowly," she said.

I was able to keep it together long enough to drive a few miles, but as soon as I pulled in the driveway, I felt myself coming undone from years of fighting uphill and feeling like I was in quicksand.

Julie ran out. She had to help me out of the car. I was a mess.

"It'll be okay, Joe," she kept saying as she ushered me inside the house.

I had trouble catching my breath. I had been avoiding the issue for seven years. And it caught up with me one day before it would have gone away for good. That's what my life felt like. No matter how fast I ran, where I went, what I did to get out of the sinkhole, something was always waiting for me to relax.

I sat down on the couch, and Julie grabbed her phone. I felt so far away, but could hear her sister on speaker phone, who was an attorney in Louisiana. My head was spinning. I thought I put Carlucci's, the bankruptcy and shitty con-men behind me.

"It'll be fine. It's okay," Julie kept saying to me.

I could hear her talking to her sister. They were asking me questions like:

How long ago did I close Carlucci's?

When did I file for bankruptcy?

And in Julie's sister's research, she found that I was one

day shy of the statute of limitations running out and now had $100,000 to pay back unless I filed bankruptcy.

Again.

I trusted Julie, and so I trusted her sister, too. I knew I was in good hands. They were both so sweet to try to comfort me. Julie's face was reassuring, and she was remarkably calm. But inside, I felt a huge void rip through my core. I instantly felt like a failure again. The weight of that $100,000 showed back up like a fat monkey and sat right back up on my shoulders.

Her sister gave us instructions. I was grateful Julie was there and taking charge of that because my head was so foggy, and it felt like it was about to explode with pressure.

The rest of the night was a blur. I took a long, hot shower, prayed, and fell into a deep sleep from pure exhaustion and crying so hard for so long. I had nothing left.

The next morning, Julie assured me she was already searching for the right bankruptcy attorney for me. There wasn't anything we could do so I just went about my normal routine. The difference was the monkey on my back and how hard I approached everything.

I went harder at the gym.

I felt a little sharper with the staff at Tortora's. I yelled a little louder.

When I could tell I was about to blow my top, I'd take a few moments by myself in the back office versus lean into someone who didn't really deserve to be leaned into. I'd catch people looking at me every once in a while. I knew why, but didn't want to explain myself to anyone.

Within the week, Julie found a highly recommended attorney only ten minutes away from the house.

"And the plan is to file bankruptcy with this guy and ensure that this time he actually files for you," she said.

We got a meeting within a matter of a day. Julie and Korey came with me. Without them, I wouldn't have made it past that day when I got the call about the court order. Without them, I would have run my car off the road. With them by my side, I was sitting in front of a real attorney who had worked with people Julie knew. He was legit and wasn't going to steal from me and leave me hanging with a $100,000 rope around my neck.

The meeting with the attorney had the same urgency as the last time I filed for bankruptcy, except this time, I was told I had to turn in my car. I couldn't own anything worth real value.

"You can clean out the car, but leave your keys at the car dealership," the attorney said.

"I don't have anything in there right now," I said and handed over the key.

And that was it. We walked out of the law offices, and I felt like I was living someone else's life. I was the general manager of this thriving restaurant. I was a world-class pizza champion and didn't own a fucking thing to my name. Not even a car.

"Well, I'll need a car to get to and from work," I said before we all climbed into Julie's car.

"We can take you to a used car dealership tomorrow," Julie said.

"Sounds like a good idea."

I was spent for the day. I didn't have the energy to do anything else, which is saying a lot for me. I'd experienced depression over the years, but nothing as bad as what I was feeling after that meeting.

The next morning, Julie, Korey, and I went to a few used car dealerships until I found something that wouldn't die on me as I drove off the lot. It was the best car I could get on the lot, and it cost me $3,000. It wasn't a lemon. I wasn't embarrassed driving it. But it wasn't something I would have picked out had the circumstances not been what they were.

I needed time by myself. We didn't open for a few hours, and nobody would be in there. I wanted space to let my head clear and the lump in my throat to dissipate. It didn't. Or maybe it couldn't.

Before we opened that night, I did what I'd done so many times before. I called Tony and Big Dave and shared the news.

They were both encouraging. Big Dave asked me if I wanted him to find me a consulting gig to lift my spirits. That was so kind of him, but my hands were so full with Tortora's as it was, so I declined. Tony reassured me that we'd be traveling again in no time, in an attempt to keep my spirits high and probably my mind occupied. Plus, any bit of extra cash flow was always welcome.

"Keep your head up, Joe," Tony said.

"I'm trying," I said.

The reality was, I was barely hanging on.

CHAPTER SEVEN

TORTORA'S

At some point early on, Joe Moore put me as the face of Tortora's. The campaign slogan was always, "Come meet Famous Joe." I was always at work. I thrived on work. I kept my head down and focused on making Tortora's as strong as I could. My strategy was to put all my energy into Tortora's as a way to make a name for myself in Alabama. I had a lot of freedom in the operational and day-to-day life of Tortora's, for which I was grateful.

We were always slammed. On the really busy days, I'd usually walk the floor, just putting out fires, helping out where I saw a need before a fire had a chance to spark.

One night, the bar was packed, with the exception of a single barstool. I saw a woman walk in whom I didn't recognize. We had a pretty steady flow of customers, so seeing someone new walk in was always exciting. She grabbed the seat at the bar and looked around. I immediately put in an order for garlic knots, knowing she was going to wait a while to get served.

It didn't take long for them to pop out. I didn't say

anything to her. I didn't introduce myself. I just placed them down in front of her on the bar and moved on to the next thing. There wasn't enough time to sit and talk to people.

I didn't find this woman striking. I wasn't attracted to her. I gave her a free appetizer because I knew she was a new customer, and I didn't want a bad review. It was something we did a lot. She wasn't a special circumstance. In hindsight, I should have explained my actions.

A few days later, I got a weird letter in the mail. It was just a bunch of rubbish, having nothing to do with me or the pizzeria. The letter mentioned a Jewish temple that I had never heard of before, along with names of plants and titles of songs. It didn't make any sense whatsoever, and I didn't give it a second thought. But on the other hand, it was so weird I knew not to toss it. I put it in a drawer in my office, just in case I needed it.

That night, the woman I gave garlic knots to came back in. I saw her walk up to the bar, and chills ran down my back by the way she looked at me. I didn't approach her. I did keep an eye on her throughout the night, and whenever I glanced over at her, she was already watching me. In my gut, I knew the creepy letter came from her.

I couldn't prove it, though, and didn't want to make a scene, so I kept my thoughts to myself. Letters continue to show up at Tortora's on a regular basis. I could never prove they were from the lady at the bar, but she continued to come in the day after a letter would get sent.

I knew it was her. I kept my distance and eventually shared my thoughts with the staff. She always sat at the bar, and I always kept my eye on my staff while she was there.

Eventually, I made my suspicions known to Joe. We agreed that we'd tell the bar staff, and if she showed up again, one of us would always have an eye on her.

In one letter, a pill was accompanied by it in a little plastic bag. We turned it into the cops and, after some research, found out it was a pill for an AIDS patient. After that, a police officer on patrol would stop in the restaurant every night to check in on us. One night, the lady was sitting in her car in the parking lot, and the officer took down her license plate and called it in just so we could have something on record.

It felt like we were just waiting for something to happen, which was a familiar feeling to my men in suits days in Danbury. I didn't like just sitting back on my heels, waiting for her to do something. She seemed like she was a little off her rocker. Crazy people tend to do crazy things. And the last thing anyone wanted was for her to lose it in Tortora's.

For the next few years, we had a great flow to Tortora's, and I was surrounded by really smart people.

After a few years of operating, Joe closed Tortora's on Sunday to give the staff a break and me a chance to reset the place. It was refreshing to have a little bit of a social life. It came at the perfect time. And when the staff started a softball team and had games on Sundays, I signed up before second-guessing it. Sunday softball games lifted my spirits a bit. I looked forward to them. It didn't matter that my outside social life involved my peers and Tortora staff!

One Sunday afternoon, we had a softball game. It was a hot, sunny day and actually really windy. By the end of the game, everyone was covered in dust. I carpooled with a buddy to the game. Before I got into his car, I took off my shoes and socks and threw them in the back. I brushed off as much dust from my pants and jersey as I could, so I didn't get his car all dirty.

I parked my car at Tortora's. As my friend pulled into the parking lot, we saw a car parked next to mine.

"What the hell?" I said under my breath.

We got closer, and I saw a woman sitting in the driver's seat. At first I didn't recognize her, and it didn't hit me who she was. When I saw her talking to herself, a switch flipped on inside. I went into instant defensive mode.

I jumped out of his car, screaming at the top of my lungs, waving my arms for her to leave the parking lot.

"What the fuck are you doing here?" I yelled. She just stared at me.

"Did you hear me?" I shouted.

She came out of her car and started reciting the latest letter.

"I know you are the one sending me those fucked up letters," I yelled.

She looked down at my feet and dropped to the ground to take off her shoes and socks. I looked at her. She was crazy. Mentally unstable for sure and probably off her medicine. She needed help but I was too pissed to care about her. She stood up and looked at me. I grabbed my phone out of my pocket, called the cops, and went inside Tortora's to wait.

I watched her from the hostess stand. She didn't do much; she just looked around and talked to herself. The police officer arrived within a matter of minutes. The stalker and letter had already been reported, so we already had a file at the station.

I was grateful to see a female cop step out of the squad car. I walked out to the parking lot, and she approached the lady.

"Ma'am, you can't be here," she said.

I didn't say anything. My friend and I stayed out of the way but had our phones ready just in case things went sideways.

"If I find out you've come back here, I will arrest you."

The lady didn't say anything. She nodded like she understood.

As the police officer came to talk to me, she looked over her shoulder, back at the lady and just then the lady plastered a huge grin on her face. The hair on my arms stood straight up and I really worried some crazy shit was going to come out to get us.

"What are you grinning at?" the police officer shouted and stormed back over to the lady. The lady did nothing.

"This is serious, ma'am. We have you on record harassing Mr. Carlucci. You don't get another warning. Leave this place right now."

The cop stood in place and waited for the lady to get back in her car and drive away.

I hoped that was the last I'd see of her. But deep down in my gut, something just wasn't right about her. I wasn't holding my breath that she was gone for good.

It was the most eventful Sunday softball day. One that I could never get out of my mind. After that, I made sure to drive by Tortora's before heading home after every game, just to make sure she wasn't in the parking lot.

She didn't show her face at Tortora's again, for which I was grateful. But I was always on alert. I'd pan the faces at the bar every night just to make sure I didn't see her. We didn't have any more crazy patrons. At least, not to that extent. We had the occasional drunk guy, just like every establishment. The staff dealt with those situations really well. After a while, it felt like my role became stagnant.

It would have been great if I could have just leaned back and coasted. I was a part of an excellent brand, but as a college drop-out I was the GM of a successful restaurant and after two years, the inner critic was loud telling me I didn't deserve it. I had a hard time turning it off. It chipped away at my self-confidence.

I wanted more. I wanted to grow it. I wanted to work with Joe on expanding a new location or even a spin-off, and only having a pizzeria. I'd bring it up to him all the time, and he'd always shoot me down. I felt like I had one hand behind my back a lot with him.

I couldn't get the thought of growing the concept out of my head, though. Having a bankruptcy attached to my name was my dirty little secret. It felt like a big fat gorilla on my back at all times, but in reality, it was a driving force for me. I felt like I had to prove myself.

It was definitely the thing that prevented me from moving out of Julie and Korey's place. What started as a temporary living situation turned out to be a permanent residence for me.

Truthfully, I loved the security and safety of the family surrounding me. Julie, Korey, and I were a family. My favorite part of the day was coming home and having a glass of wine with them.

Korey worked with Joe, and we could have honest

conversations about how frustrated I was with the growth and development of it.

"Just talk to Joe," Korey would tell me time after time.

"I *do* talk to him," I said.

"No, you guys argue," he'd laugh.

It was true. I wanted to grow Tortora's so badly, and when Joe would shake his head, I'd blow a gasket. It took a lot for Joe to open Tortora's in the first place. It wasn't fair of me to ask him to expand so soon but I needed it as a way to feel fulfilled.

Finally, I decided to shift my attention. I may not have been able to control the growth of Joe's operation. But I could control my own growth and personal development. One night, during our nightcap, I told Julie and Korey it was time to move out and find my own apartment. I needed to stand on my own two feet to prove to myself that I could after everything I'd been through.

They protested, which I figured they would. But it was something I could put my energy into. I had to do something new in my life. Julie didn't waste time. She was an amazing woman who knew so many people. She had a friend who leased apartments. She actually lived there before she and Korey bought their home. She put a call in, and within a matter of a few weeks, I was on my way over to sign a lease for an apartment that was only $800 a month. It was close to them and to Tortora's.

It felt like life was moving again, and I had that rush of excitement I needed. Julie helped me furnish it. As a minimalist, I didn't need much. I rarely went home to enjoy the luxuries of my home. I did buy a couch, table, some chairs, a bed, a dresser, and a television, but that was really it. I wasn't in a relationship at the time, so I didn't need a lot of towels or dishware. I had a few pots and pans, but nothing really extraordinary.

It was lonely at first, living by myself. I had gotten used to having Julie and Korey around. Even before I came to Alabama, I had roommates. It was the first time in a long time that I lived on my own.

During the quiet hours, usually right before I fell asleep, I could feel the weight of depression looming over me. I did what I could to brush it off and keep it at bay. When it got really loud, I'd get busy. I'd go to work to prep or do inventory.

I knew, deep down, I was eventually going to have to leave Tortora's. I wasn't done trying my hand at having my own place. The longer I worked for Joe, the worse my attitude became.

My reputation around town was that I was a cocky, loud Yankie, and to say I was living up to it would be an understatement.

I hired and fired staff for the smallest errors.

One of the ladies I hired was in her mid-20s. She was old enough to know what she wanted to do in her life, but not old enough to really go out and try it yet. Serving at Tortora's was just something she was doing while she was figuring out her next step in life. She and I had a connection right from day one. It was hard to ignore. We had a little innocent flirting happen here and there, but nothing that was probably even noticeable to anyone. I'd hold my stare with her for a few seconds longer than anyone else, and that alone made my heart beat faster. Nothing ever really happened between the two of us, but there was a spark.

When she asked for some time off of work to go visit a friend on the West Coast, I didn't think much of it. Everyone got time off. I didn't expect people to live at the restaurant like me or have nothing else in life to occupy their time with, and I let her take all the time off she wanted. We had enough staff to cover her. She wasn't sure of her return date but said within a month, she'd be back.

Her absence made me realize I was smitten with her, and I wanted to explore a relationship with her. I hated her being away and counted down the days until she returned. Finally, I got a message that she was back in town and asked to get put back in rotation for serving.

The tone of her message was very flat. She didn't offer any personal flair to her voicemail, and something about it hit me smack in the center of my heart. I called her right away and offered her a shift that night. When she got into work that night, there wasn't any sign of her being remotely interested in dating me. She wasn't cold, but it was obvious we were nothing more than colleagues in her mind. I tried to engage her in conversation about her trip, in hopes of finding the spark between us again, but it wasn't there.

I did my best to switch gears and only see her as a colleague instead of someone I was interested in having a relationship with. But I didn't do as good of a job at that as I really needed to because throughout her shift, I came down on her for any small misstep she made. And we ended up in a heated and loud argument.

We screamed at each other in the kitchen and made a huge

scene. It went on for a few minutes, but Joe came rushing in with his hands out to calm us down. He put his finger up to his lips and pointed to the dining room. I glanced out and saw folks staring back at me. I'm sure she was mortified.

"Stay out of this, Joe," I snapped.

"This is my place. You work for me and you're making a scene," he said in a hushed voice.

He ushered us both to the back patio, where nobody was seated. His eyes were narrow, and his jaw was tight. He was pissed. He was right. I did work for him. And I was making a scene. I had been trying so hard for so long to keep my shit together, but I snapped. And instead of pulling it together and calming down, I quit.

"You know what," I said calmly, realizing I was in the wrong. "I want to open my own place anyway, so I'll leave now."

"No, I'll go," she said.

Joe was surprised and probably hurt. We were both willing to walk away from Tortora's.

In the end, I walked out that night and didn't go back. I got in my car and drove straight to Julie and Korey's. They were standing in the kitchen talking to Joe.

"Okay, Joe," Julie said to her brother. "Thanks for the heads up."

She hung up the phone and gave me a look that made me feel a little less guilty. She was always comforting to me. Korey was the fixer of the family, and they guy right smack in the middle between me and Joe.

"Everything will be fine," Julie said. "I know," I said.

"Korey will fix it," she said, looking at Korey.

Korey and I locked eyes, and he shrugged. "I don't know this time, Julie. Your brother seemed pretty adamant that it's best that Joe not return."

I nodded along, knowing that was the case. "What are you going to do now?" Korey asked.

"I'll start looking for a place and investors so I can open Famous Joe's here," I said. "Just don't rush into anything," Julie said.

I smirked at her and smiled. We all knew I didn't know how *not* to rush into anything.

CHAPTER EIGHT

MADISON, ALABAMA

I IMMEDIATELY STARTED LOOKING FOR A SMALL PLACE in Madison, Alabama, where I could open a Famous Joe's of my own. Madison was 30 minutes from Tortora's, just enough space to feel like I wasn't competing against the place I loved and brought me to Alabama in the first place.

In addition to shopping for a building, I start making queries with possible investors. I needed capital. I had some guys approach me months before with an interest in getting involved in the restaurant business. They asked if I knew of a restaurant looking to expand, so I knew they were eager.

One man in particular took a liking to me. He was a high-profile individual for the defense contracts in the Huntsville area. I told him one morning after working out together what I was up to next, and he asked me to have dinner with him and his wife a few nights later.

Dinner turned into a business meeting, and he offered to gather up a group of investors on my behalf. To make it a low-risk investment, the pitch for capital was as low as $5,000 for some. Within a matter of a few weeks, I had

12 investors. Some put down $10,000, others put down $25,000 and one even put down $50,000.

The deal was that they would sit as my board of directors. I'd take $50,000 in salary, plus benefits, and have twelve percent ownership in Famous Joe's. In Alabama.

Using $225,000 to buy a restaurant isn't a lot of money. Bob used that same amount to remodel the original Famous Joe's. And the men in suits sank that much into the Danbury pizzeria before we opened it. I was excited to launch Famous Joe's in Alabama, but really worried about finding the right location with that amount of money.

One Sunday afternoon, a possible investor and I went for a drive around Madison, which was nothing but land. The purpose of our drive was to see if we could find a location for Famous Joe's. We came upon a shopping center that was brand new. It had a restaurant, but it was shut down.

It turned out that it had a second location in Knoxville, Tennessee, and sent up the manager for some training. Sadly, while in Knoxville, the manager was murdered. The guy who owned the place needed to leave Madison altogether to take care of what was happening in Tennessee, for obvious reasons.

The investors met and agreed we found a place that could work for Famous Joe's. Without hesitation, we met with the landlord and agreed to take over the lease and bought everything that was already in the restaurant for cheap. We got dishes, tables, linens, chairs, even toilet paper. We were able to do a little remodeling to be more effective for Famous Joe's.

When I wasn't working to get Famous Joe's open, I was at

the gym at 6:00 a.m. working out alongside a young lady and we sparked up a friendship. I invited her to our grand opening, which was on December 10, 2010.

It was crazy. The place was packed. My friend from the gym, Maranatha, stayed late that night, which was fun for me because up until that point, I didn't have a big social life. That night, we kissed, and a relationship quickly formed. A girlfriend was the last thing on my mind at the time.

Things really felt like they were turning for me. But the reality was there's only so long my body could take the beating. I had worked to the bone for years by that point. When I exhaled, finally, leaned back just a bit to enjoy my new relationship, it was like the adrenaline built up came to a halt and every sickness I was shoving down bubbled up to take me out.

Within a matter of a month of having Famous Joe's open, I couldn't walk. I couldn't see straight. I could barely keep my eyes open. And on New Year's Day, 2011, I wound up in the hospital. I drove myself to the ER and got seen right away. I was given fluids, antibiotics, and told to rest. There wasn't much more the doctors could do for me.

Maranatha was out of town, but when Julie called to learn of my New Year's plans, I told her where I was, and she told me to come straight over to her home. Even though Joe and I still weren't on speaking terms at that point, she insisted I rest at her place. Julie took care of me for two days.

I probably should have taken more time to rest my body, but I couldn't. I jumped back into Famous Joe's two days after my emergency room visit, still crazy burnt out but someone had to keep up with the momentum we had.

There wasn't anything around us, and the area was desperate for good pizza. We couldn't keep up with the demand. We had a long wait list, and I was working like a dog again, six days a week. I felt sick for weeks and weeks.

I finally found a manager named Quentin. He steps into the center of the business so I'm not doing everything. He had restaurant experience and knew his way around so I didn't have to micro-manage.

Meanwhile, the investors decided they wanted to have an advisor come in every single day and check in on me, review the books, write checks, and report back to the board about what was happening day-in and day-out.

With Quentin working alongside me, my workload starts to lighten up and I feel a bit more balanced. My relationship with Maranatha was going well and I'm happy for the first time in years.

And then, on April 27, 2011, an F-5 tornado hits North Alabama and destroys a lot of Madison County. I was with Quentin at Famous Joe's when the tornado sirens went off. Southern folks must have been used to the tornado warnings because we still have patrons in the dining room as reports of the tornado touching down came in.

After the last guest, we cleaned up and debated about going out to chase the storm. Maranatha called and screamed at me, so I went home to Maranatha's place instead of looking for the tornado. Good thing too, because the next morning I woke up without power, along with everyone else. But the damage to the town was incredible. Homes were leveled, people were without their belongings and cars were flipped over on top of one another.

It looked like a bomb went off—everywhere. I drove over to Famous Joe's to check the damage there and gratefully everything was still intact. However, without power, we were going to lose everything in the kitchen.

I had to do something. By 7:00 a.m. I drove to Atlanta to get a generator. We got to Home Depot and got 25 five-gallon buckets of gas cans and filled them all up with diesel. I hired an electrician on the way home to meet us at the store to hook the generator up to the back of the building.

On Friday, two days after the tornado, we were open for business. Surprisingly, we lost very little. Granted, it cost us $5,000 to open Famous Joe's. But considering we made $35,000 in sales because we were the only place open for folks to eat, it was all worth it.

People were without power for two weeks. And Famous Joe's was the only place that had power. People would wait in line to get pizza, but would use the power outlets to charge their phones while they waited. My place became a beacon of light for a lot of the community.

A few months after the clean-up of the tornado destruction, Maranatha suggested we buy a home together. I didn't have the credit, but she did. She found a place, I had some cash stored up, and we put a down payment on a home together, and we moved in.

I felt settled. Secure in my relationship. And steady on my feet.

Not long after that, it was time to compete in Naples, Italy. Maranatha came with me and saw me compete for the first time. Tony and his wife were there too. Tony and I were the only two Americans competing.

I won the title of World Fastest Pizza Maker. It didn't come with money, but it was a great honor to win the title. And to win in front of Maranatha was like the cherry on top.

When we got back home, we submitted receipts to the board, expecting to get reimbursed right away and congratulated. Instead, the board refused to pay Maranatha and me back right away. But when the television crew showed up at Famous Joes a week after my return, suddenly they were right there kissing my ass because the place blew up and we were slammed for months on end.

The following year, I had to hire more help, and I brought in two servers named Francisco and Lupe. We were always busy, and even with full-time employees, I was still working around the clock.

By this point, I had a lot of friends in the industry who were always checking in on me. One friend in particular, who had nineteen restaurants in Baltimore, became a mentor to me. He and I were on the phone seven days a week, talking about my frustrations with my board of directors and how I was never going to get out from working like a dog.

He offered to fly down for two days to check out the infrastructure, our flow, and offer insight into potential growth opportunities. While he was sitting at Famous Joe's, four members of the board came in for lunch. I introduced everyone and went on and on about how great my friend was and how successful his restaurants were in Maryland.

They hit it off and invited my colleague to a board meeting later that night. While there, they asked my friend to come in as a consultant to guide me. He turns them down, politely, but leans into the board about the changes that had to happen in order for Famous Joes to reach its potential.

I was sitting right there, watching it all unfold. Only having 12 percent ownership in Famous Joes, my hands were tied when it came to decisions that had to be made. I was grateful when he stood up for me, stating I was underpaid, working to the bone, and didn't have the proper infrastructure in place to support the sales we had. We needed more storage, more help, and newer equipment, but without the board wanting to put in more money in upgrades, Famous Joe's was as good as it was going to get. And probably, within a few years, it started to dissipate because more places were coming to Madison. Without us growing or expanding, we were looking at our own countdown.

When he left town, I knew the board wasn't going to invest in Famous Joe's growth.

The pattern of my life up to that point was that whenever a bump happened in my professional life, my personal life mirrored it. And sure enough, right around the time I learned the board of directors wasn't interested in upgrading the oven at Famous Joe's to support its potential growth, Maranatha and I started to argue a lot. We were at each other's throats and eventually would go days without talking to each other.

Something had to change. We wanted to make our relationship work. She suggested we go to couples therapy. I agreed.

One day during a therapy session, I couldn't leave my phone alone. The therapist noticed I picked it up every few seconds and asked me if I'd ever taken an ADHD test.

"Never," I said. "Why do you ask?"

"I think you should take the test online," she suggested.

We went home, and I took the test that night. The result suggested that I contact my local physician as soon as possible. It took two months to get into a doctor, but when I finally saw someone, I had to take a series of tests. It wasn't easy. The final test consisted of 300 questions, and I got so tired of it that I just started hitting the letter "A" one hundred times until I was done. I got called back the next day from a concerned individual asking if I was suicidal.

"Why do you ask?"

"You scored a 97 on your test, and we've never seen that," she said.

"A 97," I laughed. "I need to call my mom!"

Since I didn't take the test seriously, my results were skewed. I was diagnosed with ADHD, and the doctor prescribed me a pill. But I didn't want to take anything. The ADHD diagnosis made so much of my life make sense. I saw my school years differently.

Growing up in the nineties, I was put in small rooms with carpets and told I had a learning disability. Back then, I was marked differently, and that meant I had a disadvantage. ADHD was something I had even then, and nobody knew it.

I saw my drive and needed to stay busy a little differently. When I researched it more, it made me understand why I excel under pressure. I can't sit in an office for eight hours, but I can do eight hours' worth of work in an hour. I looked at it as an advantage. I didn't see ADHD as a scarlet letter or a thorn in my side.

And learning about ADHD made the challenges in my relationship make a little more sense. Being diagnosed with ADHD wasn't the straw that broke the camel's back in my relationship, but it helped me see how different we were. We agreed it wasn't working, but really wanted it to.

When the opportunity came to travel to Dubai with Siler to throw pizza at the Ferrari World theme park later that month, I jumped all in. Maranatha came with me, and we had the time of our lives. We decided to look at the trip as a fresh start for us. To our future. And when I wasn't tossing, and she wasn't working on her laptop in the hotel room, we took advantage of everything Dubai had to offer.

We rode camels and Jeeps in the sand. We went to the race track. We cooked meals in the hotel most of the time to save money and made ourselves right at home.

When we came back, it wasn't long before we finally came to the conclusion that we were just too different to last. While we complemented each other in beautiful ways, the differences in how we approach life made it really hard to see a future together.

But God had other plans for us. We had a home together. Neither one of us was really interested in leaving. But when Maranatha found out she was pregnant, we decided to continue living together until our daughter was born. Life changed overnight. I was so scared. I kept thinking, *I'm not going to be a good dad.* I always wanted a kid, but I didn't think I was ready.

Even though I had massive doubts about my ability to step up and be there for our baby, I was right next to Maranatha for every appointment or whenever she needed or wanted something. I wanted to prove to myself that I could be a good partner and a great father.

And then, God showed me something to help me see the type of dad I'd become: A young girl comes into Famous Joe's one afternoon with her family. She's bald and wearing a scarf on her head. I talked to the family and learned that she has cancer, and they were having some financial difficulties getting her treatment paid for.

Something stirred deep inside me at that moment. It wasn't the fire or the light switch I'd felt before when driving by something. This was deeper. Almost primal. An instinct kicked in for this young girl, and I was moved beyond anything I'd ever felt before.

I wanted to help. I decided to put together a fundraising event to help this young girl. I called a few people I knew in the community who could donate silent auction items for patrons to bid on. I got a baseball and even a car donated. The press came out of the woodwork to shine a light on our community fundraiser, and together, we raised $15,000 to help her and her family pay for her cancer treatment.

After watching all of that around me, I knew I was going to be a solid dad. I'd be the type of dad my daughter could come to no matter what. I'd treat her like a princess, but help her grow up to always know she could do everything herself. I wanted her to be strong, smart, kind, but also fierce.

When Valentina was born, Maranatha and I agreed we would spend the next year of our lives devoted to our daughter. We agreed not to date and to put our full focus on her. She moved out, and I kept our home. But several times after work, I'd go over to her new place and sleep on the couch to help with night-time feedings. When I wasn't there, I asked my staff to support Maranatha and Valentina. We had a lot of help. Valentina was loved by everyone from the moment she arrived. Everyone I called a family member had a role in her new life.

Months went by, and life caught a rhythm. I had a successful pizzeria that I knew wasn't going to grow, but wasn't showing signs of slowing down. I was a new father and loved my daughter more than anyone else on the planet. My house was a shrine to Valentina. I framed the scrubs I was wearing when Valentina was born. It had her footprint on it. I hung it in my bedroom. It was just one of many moments I framed with Valentina's face on it.

And Maranatha and I felt like we were in a good place.

One night, it hit me. I wanted my daughter to have a father and mother under the same roof. It dawned on me that if I wanted to get back together with Maranatha, even become husband and wife one day, I was going to have to pull out all the stops.

And that's exactly what I did.

I went out of my way to give Maranatha the biggest surprise. I reached out to her cousin through social media and asked if she had any pictures of Maranatha's dad because he passed away a few years before. Her dad was in the Vietnam War. I wanted to gather all his military memorabilia, medals, and documents, but I needed a family member to sign a consent form to have it sent to me.

The cousin lets Maranatha's mom know what I'm up to, and she agrees to sign the form for me. I told Lupe and Francisco what I was doing, and they covered Famous Joe's.

I got in my car and drove from Madison, Alabama, to New York to get the form signed.

Because they were helping me, I wanted to give something in return. Before I started my 16-hour drive, I grabbed the frame of my scrubs with Valentina's footprint on it to give to Maranatha's grandmother.

I drove all day and night. I got the form signed and was given a photograph of Maranatha's dad in front of the American flag from his early days in the military. I slept for a few hours on her grandma's couch and then drove all the way back.

I submitted the form as quickly as possible and didn't have to wait more than a week to get all of the medals her dad was awarded while serving in the Vietnam War. Meanwhile, I placed the photos of her dad in a shadow box next to the American flag. I wrote a letter to her and then hired a gentleman to translate it into Korean.

I didn't stop there. Maranatha's mom told me she played the piano when she was little. I found a piano online for a decent price and arranged to have it delivered on a Sunday when she was on a road trip with Valentina. She wasn't going to be gone for long.

My friends and I hurried and got everything set up in her family room. I placed photos of Valentina on the piano, alongside the medals, the shadow box, the letter, a little video I made, and then finally surrounded it all with rose petals.

I went all out and then went home and waited for her to call. A few hours went by before my phone rang. I picked up, hoping for the best. Instead, it went the other way.

"When are you getting the piano out?" she asked.

CHAPTER NINE

THE DECLINE OF FAMOUS JOE'S AND THE HUSTLE CULTURE

It was obvious she didn't want to get back together. But the way she handled it hurt me pretty deeply. I went to get the piano out the next day and told her from that point on, our relationship was about Valentina. Like many other people in our situation, it all came down to the child. We weren't married. Sadly, we dove into a big custody battle. She wanted full custody, but I wanted split custody.

Maranatha had a great government job, and she could afford the best attorney in town.

During that time, I couldn't see Valentina at all. It only lasted two weeks, but it felt like years. Each day, I could feel depression weighing down on me more and more. My happiness and worth as a man were 100 percent wrapped around my daughter. Nothing else mattered.

Famous Joe's became something I did. Since Valentina, everything revolved around her. Everything I did was for her. I even had tattoos of her face, name, and birthdate on my body. I had my car wrapped with her face and birthday.

While I still had responsibilities at Famous Joe's, and we stayed open the entire time I slugged through the custody battle, the pizzeria did have a little wobble. The restaurant was still stable but there was a slight decrease in revenue. Not by much but enough for the board to notice.

After the advisor would report my sales for the day back to the board, I'd get a nasty phone call reminding me that I had 12 investors who wanted to see a return on their investment. And they'd go as far as to tell me it wasn't appreciated that my personal life had gotten in the way of Famous Joe's.

I didn't even care. I didn't have the energy to argue or fight. I understood that they didn't like that I wasn't grinding it out every day in the kitchen. I was still able to take care of my staff and pay them what they were owed.

I always wanted to take care of them. We had created such a deep bond and trusted one another. I hoped they understood why I was preoccupied. One afternoon early on in the custody battle, a staff member offered to babysit Valentina when Maranatha was working. My heart could have burst on the spot. Lupe was an angel to me. I grabbed her and held her and started crying on her shoulder.

"God, thank you, Lupe," I got out. She held me and let me sob for a bit.

I called Maranatha immediately and prayed she would agree to my request. God was shining down on me that day. Maranatha needed the help as much as I wanted someone I trusted watching over my daughter. Lupe started babysitting for us the next morning. For the next 10 days, I was able to learn about the day-to-day care of my daughter. I'd text Lupe and ask for photos or just random updates about what

Valentina was doing. My focus was not on patrons or making money. I went through the motions to keep the board of directors off my back, but my muscle memory took over as my mind was focused on how I was going to stay in my daughter's life.

After I got the piano out of her place, I learned Maranatha was in a new relationship. She was in love with someone else. Someone else who could provide her with things that I couldn't.

Picturing that man raising my daughter fueled my fire to fight for my rights as my daughter's father. I couldn't imagine life without her. When that thought crept into my mind, I'd find myself clenching my jaw tight, and my shoulders would tighten up into my ears. I had to force myself to calm down and shake off the fear of losing her.

While Lupe was helping us take care of Valentina, I asked my attorney to lift the restriction on not being able to see her. Gratefully, that ended after two weeks, and I got Valentina on the weekends throughout the summer.

Before I knew it, the time for our court appearance came. I dressed in my nicest suit and tie. I got as much sleep as I could and got to the courthouse with plenty of time. I watched Maranatha enter the room with her attorney. Our eyes locked, and it was like I was looking at a woman I didn't even know. I was still in disbelief that our relationship had come to this.

Maranatha never wanted to go to court. But I couldn't let her have full custody, so court was our only option. She took the stand and everything seemed cordial. And then I got up on the stand and her attorney tore me apart.

She brought up my ADHD diagnosis, the fact that I was heading to LA later that day to do a show called The Taste. She brought up my tattoos. I was painted as a bad father. All they saw was a dude from New York with big tattoos, and they attacked me because of my diagnosis. It didn't matter that I had a letter from a three-star general about my character, the mom of the young girl I helped fundraise cancer treatment for, or the mayor of the city. I think Jesus himself could have written a letter, and it still wouldn't matter.

It was heartbreaking, and when I locked eyes again with Maranatha, we both started crying. The woman I loved for years was sitting there, not wanting any of this to happen.

As soon as the trial ended, I got out of there as quickly as possible. I couldn't look at Maranatha on the way out. I do what I can to get my mind straight and focus on the upcoming taping of a reality cooking show called The Taste. When I was asked to come on the show, I told the producer about my daughter. And she thought it would make for a great storyline. Maranatha agreed to let Lupe care for Valentina while I taped the show in Los Angeles. The three of us were on a plane to L.A., not long after our horrific showdown in the courtroom.

Not surprisingly, I didn't do well on *The Taste*. In fact, I was the first one eliminated from it. And the three of us were back on a plane heading home the next morning.

Weeks went by and I didn't hear a thing. Until finally, I got a call from Maranatha. "Did you see the email?" she asked.

"What email?"

"You get Valentina every other Wednesday and every other weekend."

I dropped to the floor. I was shattered. I bawled. To the point I lost my breath and had to force air out of my lungs. My heart felt like it was being ripped out of my chest. I closed my eyes because the room started to spin. Minutes went by before I was able to collect myself. I calmed myself down and looked at the phone. Maranatha was talking. I held the phone up to my ear and heard her say, "I don't want to do this. I don't want to fight this. I don't want you to lose your home."

"I'll die before I lose my home. Or my daughter."

I hung up the phone and realized I was sitting at rock bottom. I reached it. I felt like I was losing everything and everyone and nobody was on my side. Life was doomed and nothing I did was ever going to mean anything to anyone. The thoughts going through my head were not healthy or uplifting.

Depression had me in a chokehold, and the only thing I was looking forward to was seeing my daughter that weekend. When I picked up Valentina for the night, Maranatha asked if I could talk. Her boyfriend was holding Valentina behind her. My skin crawled.

"I have an idea," she said.

I followed her inside and we sat down at her kitchen table. I let her talk.

"I don't want to fight anymore. I have stipulations," she said.

And before I could say anything, she went on to list out what she wanted.

Maranatha asked that I pay for half her attorney fees, always able to claim Valentina on her taxes, and everything removed from my car that referenced Valentina.

"I'd rather pay an attorney than give you a dime," I said.

I wasn't in a compromising frame of mind. I took Valentina out of her boyfriend's arms and left without saying anything else. I called my friend in Baltimore and told him everything. He begged me to listen to his advice and told me to agree to her terms.

"Joe, you'll see your daughter much more this way. Trust me." So, I did.

I called Maranatha the next day and said, "I agree."

"Ok, great. I'll call my attorney and set it up," she said.

A few days later, we met at her attorney's office to sign paperwork. I get put on a payment plan of $2,000 a month for six months to cover her legal fees, plus child support of $1,100 a month. I couldn't focus on the amount because I was so thrilled that I got my daughter whenever I wanted. I agreed to everything and walked out of the office, with Valentina coming home with me for the next week.

Meanwhile, Famous Joe's wasn't my main priority, which pissed off the investors.

The board was so tired of my personal life getting in the way of their bottom line, so they threatened to replace me. One afternoon, I got a call from a friend of mine who told me the board wanted to replace me with him. That day, I went into Famous Joe's, and the advisor was already there waiting for me. I was told that we were closing for remodeling. The plan was to tell the public and my staff we were only closing for two weeks. But the investors were done. They weren't ever planning on opening the doors again.

"You can't do that. I live here, and these people are part of my family. You can't do that to them," I said.

"That's what's happening," an investor said.

That was the end of Famous Joe's. It was May 2013.

I brought my close staff into the office to let them know what was happening. I assured them I'd be there for them and do whatever they needed me to do.

There was one bill still left unpaid, and the board expected me to pay it. But without any income, my hands were tied. And they kept calling for weeks on end asking me for the $1,200. But that's what I owed in child support and couldn't even pay that.

I had all the same bills, and now no money coming in. The custody battle cost so much for us both, and I had to pay half of what Maranatha owed. Nothing popped for me after The Taste. And I hadn't been in a competition or taken a consulting gig since before all the attorney fees started piling up. On top of it all, I was still paying off my mom for Carlucci's.

I was drowning in debt. Bills. Every time I turned around, I had to pay someone something. Tony was calling and checking in on me all the time, which was a beacon of light in my life at the time. He even sent me cash to keep me afloat. It killed me to accept it, but I had the weight of the world on my back and felt like the rug was ripped out from underneath me.

When Famous Joe's closed, my eyes opened up wide. I was able to see the friends I thought I had weren't anything but foes. I assumed everyone who came into Famous Joes and sat at the bar and said hello to me around town was a friend but when the restaurant closed, I didn't feel anyone cared about me.

I started to see myself on an island all alone. Depression came knocking. Hard. Loud. It was dark. And it just kept getting dark. That's the thing about depression, though. It was always playing tricks on me, and every moment was different. One second, I'd have a thought that the world was a better place without me, and the next minute, my friend who owns the gym I was working out at asked me if I wanted to clean it for him at night. And what he was willing to pay me was the exact amount I owed in child support.

It wasn't the first time I played the role of a janitor. When I worked at the hospital, I cleaned up in scarier places than a sweaty locker room. I didn't have any pride left. I took the gig and paid Maranatha.

Then I learned that a private school was looking for someone to make lunches for them. They didn't have a cafeteria and needed help right away. Even though I didn't have a home permit, I called them up, introduced myself and explained my circumstance and laid out a quick menu of chicken fingers, pizza, and cold sandwiches. I got that gig too and started making 100 lunches every day in my kitchen with a kid I hired part-time. It took hours to prepare everything by lunchtime.

An old customer, who grew into a friend, called me and offered me a regular catering gig. He was a pharmaceuticals rep who always had meetings he needed food for.

Between the school and the catering gigs, I was able to stay afloat for the next nine months.

However, I always searched for consulting gigs and

competitions that could garner some additional cash. But the debt, child support, and attorney fees were too much each month. I was robbing Paul to pay Peter, and sometimes even he got stiffed. I wasn't paying my mortgage or my electricity bill. To keep food on the table and gas in the car, I started selling furniture.

I sold the washer and dryer, kitchen table and chairs, and Valentina's furniture, including her bed, which she adored. I hated having to sell it, but we needed the cash. When I had Valentina and a catering gig, Lupe and Francisco would watch Valentina for me.

I didn't particularly like the private school job but to make it work I had to find a bigger space and a legit kitchen where my permit covered. I found a restaurant two miles from the school that was looking for someone to rent out their kitchen space in the morning. It would have worked perfectly.

I could cook in the morning and still keep the food warm during transportation.

I didn't want to rush into anything, and I had a quick trip planned to New Jersey, so I didn't sign a lease right away.

My friend in New Jersey asked me to come up for the weekend to throw pizza with his sons, who were already amazing competitors. I jumped at the chance to get out of Alabama for the weekend and told the young man working with me that he had a small order to deliver to the school on the Friday that I was gone.

He assured me he could handle it. So, when the school administrator emailed me, complaining that the food was cold, I was surprised.

When I got back to town, I hurried and went over to talk to the landlord. I was pretty raw in our meeting. I laid my guts out on the table like he was a scavenger looking through my remains. I wouldn't be surprised if he just told me to leave, but instead, he said he liked me and my transparency and wanted to transfer the lease to me with one condition.

"What's that?" I laughed.

The landlord wanted my friend from Baltimore to stay on the lease for one year. He didn't have a problem doing that, and was helping me negotiate the terms of the lease, so it wasn't a surprise to him that he would be asked to be on the lease for a year.

"That's great, but I don't have the cash to do it," I said.

"Well, if you can get it together, I could do it this week. You'd need a two-month security deposit. It's $6,000 total and there's a three-year lease available," he said.

I started going to quick loan shops to get cash, but hated every second of it. Knowing I was adding to my debt pile didn't make sense, but I wanted to see where this road went. Eventually, I secured $6,000 and went back to see the landlord to sign the lease. The first call I made was to my buddy who owned the gym. I wasn't going to be able to clean for him on one side of town when I had a kitchen 30 minutes away in Athens, Alabama.

I was doing my best to get into a positive state of mind. I had made a big leap of faith, trusting I was being led down this particular path for a purpose. I just didn't know what that purpose was at the moment.

I moved everything out of my home kitchen and into the kitchen in Athens just before I had to get on a plane to head to the Pizza Expo in Las Vegas. The kid who worked for me part-time was left in charge again.

And just like before, I told him what he was responsible for, and I assumed he could be trusted to get hot food transported two miles to the school.

When I got back from Las Vegas, he and I delivered food to the school on a Friday. A little while later, I got an email from the principal of the school letting me know they canceled their orders with me claiming the food was cold.

I was disappointed but I understood. It didn't make the sting any less potent though. I was sitting in my car, in my driveway reading that email. I looked up at my front door and saw a tag on it. It was a notice from the electric company letting me know they turned off my power.

I was a few thousand dollars behind on my bill. I had no choice but to call Maranatha and tell her I couldn't pick up Valentina for a little bit. And I finally let her in on what was happening.

She was sympathetic and told me to hold off on child support for a bit, which actually made me feel worse. And that's when the darkest hour of my life took place.

What the fuck are you doing, you worthless piece of shit. Why even bother?

Just end it.

I sat on the floor of my bedroom, crying uncontrollably. I looked up at my wall and saw a photo of Valentina. Seeing her picture calmed me down. Her face gave me all the motivation I needed.

After a while, I picked myself off the floor, fell asleep, and stayed asleep for a few hours.

The next morning, I went to my men's prayer group I had been going to. I told them what was going on. I asked for prayers and admitted to my dark hour the night before.

"You're loved, Joe," he said. "Thank you."

"You have people," he said.

"It doesn't always feel like that."

"You just have to ask for help."

I went to work and kept my head down, just putting one foot in front of the other. When I got home that night, my power was back on. My friends in my prayer group paid for it. And I made a promise to myself that I would never return to that dark place again. If I ever felt that helpless again, I'd call a friend before I let that inner demon get me like that. I knew I had people in my life who loved me. When I was in the right frame of mind, I knew exactly who I was, what I brought to the world, and who I needed to carry on for.

I got Valentina the next day. I couldn't offer her much at that point in my life, but I gave her all I had.

CHAPTER TEN

JOE'S WORLD FAMOUS

I HAD A KITCHEN. IT WAS THIRTY MINUTES AWAY FROM Famous Joe's. And luck had turned toward me. Local friends showed up out of the woodwork to help me fix it up.

I needed an updated oven first and foremost and was grateful the oven company asked me to do some consulting with them gave me a great discount on a state-of-the-art oven. That was an easy decision to make.

Next, the point of sale company offered me a computer system for free, and I got chairs donated by a friend.

I was even introduced to a generous benefactor who offered to loan me $5,000 to open the doors, and he died without anyone knowing he gave me the money or before I could pay him back.

Finally, I decided to call it Joe's World Famous. Within a month of signing the lease, I opened the doors. The place does well from day one. The problem was always the credit card loans with the 40 percent interest rates. I was still robbing Paul to pay Peter and would have to accept handouts from friends to put gas in my car and food on my own table.

Joe's World Famous was paying for itself, except for me. I wasn't making any money.

A year into it, a guy walks into Joe's World Famous and tells me he wants to help me. He read all about me and said he could help me put up a sign and get an ice machine. He didn't want reimbursement right away. He just wanted to support me, and I accepted any help I could get. Having the sign up definitely helped bring more traffic in.

My loans and debt were at an all-time high, maybe $100,000. Maybe more. I had to find a way to make more money. Joe's World Famous was busy and getting busier with every reality show gig I got, but I wanted something more.

At the time, restaurant owners were catering out using food trailers. It gave us opportunities we didn't otherwise have, and I went in on it too. I got another loan to buy a pizza trailer and immediately saw an additional income stream. I hitched it to my truck and started catering immediately. But first, I had to get more help.

I called Lupe and Francisco, and they jumped at the chance to help me out and earn some extra cash.

I started to see things coming together. I was making more. Which meant I could pay back more. But so much damage had already been done. I needed help. As year two came around for Joe's World Famous, I looked for a partner. I wanted someone who could put some money in, so I could start seeing a salary again. I needed to turn things around with Maranatha and finally pay off my mom.

My relationship with Maranatha was civil, but I owed her $8,000 in back child support money.

One day, Valentina told me that she was a little sad and

that she had to move away. It came out of the thin air and shocked the shit out of me.

"What do you mean, honey?" I asked her, hugging her.

"We're looking at homes. Mom said."

I reassured her that no matter where she was, I'd be there for her. We watched a funny movie that night, and I made sure she wasn't sad when I took her to school the next day. But as soon as I saw her walk inside the building, I called Maranatha to get the full scoop. They were moving twenty-five miles away from me.

"You can't do this to me again," I said.

"Joe, you owe so much money. You still haven't paid off my legal fees. You owe me a ton in child support."

"I can't afford child support, or I would pay it!" I yelled.

"Then we have to go back to court."

"Yes. Let's. Take a look at my books. You'll see. I can't afford $1,100."

We had to revisit court, which just added more weight to my back and more pressure on my heart. I felt like I was drowning again, but we agreed on $600 a month in child support. It was the silver lining in a long line of bills I had to pay. I could deal with $600 a month.

I kept my head down, took on as many catering gigs as I could, hustled harder. More. More. More. And finally, I got a lead on a potential partner. I was introduced to a patron's son who wanted 49% ownership.

I'd been bullshitted to one too many times, but I knew I needed someone to come in if Joe's World Famous was going to make it. I still had the rest of the second year, and the third year left on the lease. I set up a meeting at Joe's World

Famous and got sold the moon. The guy tells me everything and anything I could possibly want in a partner. He's willing to put money in right away, has a legal contract, has some accounting knowledge, and is able to do the books and even the taxes.

I'd be the front of the house, and he'd be the back. It's what every restaurant owner needs. I couldn't be everything and do everything. But I was great at running the kitchen, doing the press, marketing, and keeping people happy. The rest of it, the legal and accounting pieces, could be someone else's hat.

Right out of the gate, I saw a regular salary. Seeing money hit my account, on the day we agreed on, for the amount we agreed on, was refreshing. I logged into my bank account first thing Friday morning and felt panic rush up my back as I waited for my account to load. I feared the worst. And exhaled when I saw the increase in my balance.

I started to breathe again—immediately started paying my child support and looked for more ways to bring in more business. I wanted more. Again. I had some wind back in my sails and I knew I could get out of this shitstorm of back debt.

I was on a high. I got on *The F Word* with Gordon Ramsay to try to get a Guinness World Record for the largest pizza spin. There's so much press surrounding the event. I knew it was all for Ramsey, but it felt cool, nonetheless. I did my thing, spun pizzas, and got down on the ground and wowed the crowd. It felt amazing to be in front of people again.

I won the Guinness World Record for Spinning the

Largest Pizza in 2017, and I knew it was going to do something good to my business. It felt bigger than the others. Joe's World Famous was packed for months after that because people saw me on the show.

We were making hand-over-fist, and there was a line out the door. We couldn't keep up with the demand, and my business partner just cracked. He couldn't handle the speed or the demand. He left in the middle of the day, and I was there to pick up the pieces.

It was Joe's World Famous after all, and I should have learned by then that I couldn't count on anyone to perform the same way I could. My expectations of others were incredibly high, always have been. But my name was on the door again, and after being on TV again, I wanted Joe's World Famous to measure up to the expectations people had when walking through the front door.

He definitely wasn't the man or business partner he made himself out to be, or I thought he was. As soon as we could part ways, I was going to. But I still had one more year on the lease of the place. And my heart was being pulled into the pizza trailer. Something about it just felt right. I knew that was how I was going to get out from under the mounting debt and crushing bills.

Gratefully, we were still on a high from The F Word, and our catering business was at an all-time high. Everyone wanted pizza from the guy on The F Word. I was accepting weddings, anniversaries, parties, corporate events, and everything in between. I said yes to any event where I could park the trailer for a few hours and make a shit ton of cash.

One afternoon, I got a call from the booking producer

at Master Chef, and she invited me to a tryout in Nashville. While I was auditioning, we got a catering job for an anniversary party from an acquaintance of mine who was an executive in the area. He had been following me for a while and wanted to support me. He loved our pizza and was excited to have us cater for him.

Since I was gone, I didn't handle the order. And sadly, my staff dropped the ball. I was mortified to learn we weren't going to be able to deliver his order on such an important occasion for him. Gratefully, the client was understanding.

My focus shifted from the brick-and-mortar to the trailer after The F Word. I knew an opportunity when I saw one, and I was riding that wave until it dried up. Since my partner always took care of our books and the taxes, I assumed he was still doing that. And then my salary started to decrease. And then I stopped getting paid altogether. Our lease was almost up, and we both knew the restaurant wasn't going to make it. But the trailer could. I wanted to sell it all together, get out, get away from my partner, and start a food truck from scratch. Instead, I settled for my partner selling his half to someone else, who promised me he'd help me get catering gigs for the truck.

We agreed on the new arrangement, closed the brick-and-mortar, and I found a kitchen to prep in at a gas station in the middle of nowhere. It wasn't in a great part of town. I witnessed many drug deals on my way into the kitchen. I left them alone, and they left me alone.

As much as I wanted life to be different, it was just one guy offloading his debt to someone else. I was still left with a shit ton of loans and back taxes that my partner never paid.

The weight was pressing down on me, and oftentimes, it was hard to take a deep breath. I was running on adrenaline and shocked I hadn't keeled over and had a heart attack. The stress was at its highest.

One day, I met two people who had a pizza food truck and had a contract with The Arsenal. They came in and asked me about my oven. We became friends. I told them I was getting out of the brick-and-mortar business and wanted to just do the food truck business. They said they were getting out of the food truck business and were happy to help me. They held my hand and threw weddings at me, and got into Redstone Arsenal, a United States Army base close to Huntsville.

I raked in $2,000 there three days a week and only do a two-hour shift. It was hard work. More physical than the restaurant, but I loved it.

I made a lot of contacts while selling pizzas at The Arsenal. Many turned into private catering gigs. And whenever I saw the gentleman we botched a catering order for, I made sure to go out of my way to talk to him. He was a great supporter of ours and I wanted to keep it that way.

He was always willing to talk about my long-term plans. I asked him to dinner to talk about an idea I had in the back of my mind about opening another pizzeria.

During our conversation, he asked me point-blank how much it would cost for me to get a place open.

"I could probably open the doors for $50,000," I said.

"Your risk-to-reward would be enormous if you hit," he said. "I just have to get cash to do it this time," I said.

I appreciated the friendship and conversation, but then

put the idea of another pizzeria back in the corner of my mind. I dove head first into the food truck industry. I drove within twenty miles of Huntsville for orders. One time I drove to Jackson, Mississippi but only sold two pizzas. I didn't leave Alabama after that. I didn't really know how to manage it, but I gave it my all. It never felt like enough though.

There was always a give-and-take. I was hiding my car to avoid it being repossessed by the bank because I hadn't paid it in months. But I was able to find a new kitchen and negotiate a crazy cheap lease for only $550 a month. I had to find balance every single day and look for the light in individual moments or those dark thoughts and that inner demon would have gotten me.

I was a 40-year-old, single father, who barely saw his daughter, with more debt than I knew what to do with. I was on national television shows but hiding my car.

People wanted to help, but didn't know how. Hell, I didn't know how to tell people to help me. "Get me a catering gig," I'd laugh.

It was the only thing I could think of.

I kept doing the truck, selling pizza, and eventually branched out into more Italian cuisine, all throughout Alabama. I'd see Valentina at night because the truck didn't run at night. I had help on the weekends and when I had events, but otherwise it was just me.

The food truck community was my saving grace. I learned I had a family within these businesses. We talked about events, which ones to go to and which ones to avoid. We tagged each other on social media and really lifted each other up.

But the truck business itself was struggling. The physical demands in and of itself were more than I anticipated.

And then COVID hit, and my life changed.

COVID was a blessing in disguise. I got down on my knees and thanked God for what COVID did for my business. Everyone was at home, and I had a mobile restaurant essentially. They could social distance but still have the thrill of take-out.

At first, nobody wanted to go to a restaurant. And I took advantage of that. I started parking in front of the commissary, a food preparation station. People found me there. And as the food truck business took off, the longer COVID went on, the harder we rallied as a community.

Soon, neighborhoods started calling us and asking us to come out for the day. I'd go from 11:00 a.m. to 1:00 p.m. for lunch, go back to the commissary and reload and go to a different neighborhood at night. I never went to the same subdivision more than once in the same month. I was doing a lot of business, and the other food trucks and I started tagging each other online, letting each other and neighbors know where we were going to be and the hours we were there.

If I was going to a neighborhood on a Wednesday, I'd announce it on Tuesday and offer pre-orders Tuesday night, but have an automatic shut-off time to close pre-orders. I woke up every morning, excited to see how many pre-orders.

We'd sell at least 75 pizzas during lunch. We'd sell 150 pizzas at night.

I'd talk to a friend in the food truck every morning and every night to talk about how crazy the business was.

Regardless of how many pre-orders I had the night before in a neighborhood, I'd always blow out and sell out.

I couldn't keep up. I didn't have to go more than fifteen miles to sell out. I started racking up the money. I did it for six months—paid off my mom, most of the loans, and Maranatha. Plus, I had $60,000 in savings.

When it first started, I didn't see Valentina and it killed me. I went three months without seeing her. But I knew the whole time, she was healthy and safe, and everything I was doing was for her benefit. I was getting out of debt, paying off huge loans in one swipe. And I was a better man and could be a better father once I was out from under the mountain I got myself buried under.

Surprisingly, during COVID, I reconnected with a high school sweetheart, and she and I talked all the time. Her friendship was really beneficial to me during quarantine.

Once the COVID-19 lockdown mandate was lifted, Valentina would join me on the truck when she was done with school. She'd box pizza and hand drinks out. She'd help me clean the truck. She learned how to handle cash and credit cards. As summer went on and the business slowed down, she brought her Barbies. And she'd be out in the neighborhood mixing it up with other girls, hustling on her own. She'd make trades or even sell her Barbies.

When people went back to restaurants and the novelty of having a food truck in the subdivision wore off, we stopped showing up. And my business partner and I sat down and agreed we wanted different things. I was ready to get out of the hot truck, sweating my face off, drenched from the oven. He wanted to continue down that road, which was easy for him to say because he was never on the truck with me. But I was ready to try my luck, one last time, at a brick-and-mortar.

We sold the truck to a retired couple in Texas. They came down and bought the trailer. We took that money and paid back a good amount of our debt as business owners, and I finally felt the chains break free from my body. A load was lifted, and I sat in my car, which the bank couldn't take away, and sobbed.

I let that feeling of freedom wash over me. I called my high school sweetheart and told her the news.

I didn't have any more partners. I had more money in the bank than I ever had before. And I knew exactly what I wanted to do next in my life.

I called Maranatha.

"I'm going to open a pizzeria," I said when she answered. I could hear Valentina in the background.

"Oh yeah?"

"I want to call it Valentina's," I said loudly so Valentina could hear me.

"Let's ask Valentina first," she said. "Is that okay with you?"

"YES," Valentina shouted.

With her blessing, my next chapter started. And so did Valentina's.

CHAPTER ELEVEN

VALENTINA'S

VALENTINA WAS SO EXCITED ABOUT MY DECISION TO name a pizzeria after her. I knew in my heart this was it for me. If Valentina's didn't work, I was done. I didn't want to think about a Plan B, but in the back of my mind, if I thought for a second the place was going under, I was going to sell it and walk away from the industry once and for all.

Where I was going to open Valentina's was an easy decision for me to make. I had a cheap lease on a commissary really close to where I lived. I wasn't going to waste time searching for something new. I knew I wanted to turn the commissary into a pizzeria.

I didn't have a lot of advisors around me at the time. I was well seasoned on what I needed to do to get Valentina's open. I did want a sounding board to talk over my ideas with. Tony had always been there for me to discuss the industry. But I wanted someone to talk to who knew the local area.

I reached back out to the executive I met at The Arsenal, who had become a good friend and even a mentor.

I told him I had the $50,000 saved, and he offered to be a sounding board for me whenever I needed it.

He wasn't asking to get in on Valentina's with me. He wasn't asking to be an investor. He was guiding me. He didn't want anything from me. But he was willing to give me his time and energy to walk with me on this next adventure.

Even though I already told Valentina I was moving forward with my plan, I was so scared. I couldn't get both feet to stand firm on the same first step. I had a big confidence dip. I called a few friends to help me get my mind right, and every single one of them said the same thing.

Joe. Do it. Whatever you need. I'm there. You have to do it.

Valentina actually helped me get over the hump. She was so proud to tell her friends about this new place, her famous pizza dad was going to open with her name. She took out her phone, recorded a video, and sent it out. She announced Valentina's to all her friends. And made the decision that we'd not sell pineapple. Ever.

Watching her take action so confidently, proudly, and fiercely reminded me of why I do what I do and who I do it for. So, I went to work.

I bought a lot of used-equipment online but bought the best oven money could buy. The chairs and tables were local. I had friends with trucks and trailers help me run around town to pick-up material for the pizzeria. I put in every last penny I had saved into getting everything as perfect as I could.

I wanted to keep the menu really tight, so all we made was pizza. It was my idea to keep our overhead low, keep the inventory budget-friendly, and I even limited our hours.

I found a graphic designer online and hired her to do

our logo, signage, and menu. It didn't take more than two months to get the doors open. And then, on October 9, 2020, during COVID, I opened my little 40-seat pizzeria. We followed the rules and had people sit six feet apart. I didn't have any expectations for sales that night. I was nervous but put on a brave face for Valentina.

Thankfully, we were busy and saw good sales right out of the gate.

I was gutted with nasty remarks from so-called friends and customers all night. I don't even think my family believed Valentina's was going to make it based on their reactions.

Dude. This location sucks.

Do you think you'll make it work this time?

How did you make this happen? Are you stealing money?

I responded to every comment as graciously as I could, but inside, I was cussing everyone out.

Asshole. Get out of here.

The location was off the beaten path. It was across from a cornfield. It was a risk. But something about it felt right. And I was ready to be on a path of least resistance. And opening Valentina's was the easiest opening I experienced.

Granted, it wasn't a huge place. As much as I wanted Valentina's to be smooth-sailing, and nothing but black ledgers every day, we had massive bumps but great sales. I kept my head down, worked hard, and kept the staff small so my overhead stayed low.

For the first six months, I kept getting hit with tax letters. I thought my old partner was paying them because he was handling the books. So, the first big surprise came with having to get the old tax cleaned up. And once that disappeared, I started saving money again.

Life was different. I owned Valentina's on my own. We had a great clientele. And the best part about it was that Valentina and I saw each other all the time. And even more, she started showing interest in getting involved in the pizza business and learning how to make dough and toss dough. We'd play around in the kitchen together.

"Dad, how do I get a record like you?"

"What kind of record do you want?"

"Whatever kind you have," she laughed.

I had two Guinness World Records by that point. The highest toss and the largest pizza spin. We decided that Valentina would try her luck at the highest toss for girls ages 9-11. I did some research, and we sent in an entry form to the Kids Guinness World Records, requesting they come out to record Valentina.

We start practicing after school for weeks. They responded and sent criteria. I had to get a city official and a film crew. So we decided to do it on the one-year anniversary of the store opening. I pulled out all the stops.

I got a waterslide placed out front of the shop. We invited all her friends and, of course, her mom and stepdad. When the news crew arrived, we went out in front of the 80-foot by 20-foot mural on the side of the building. Valentina's face is all over it. She got three attempts. She stood in front of her painting and threw the pizza dough in the air. It couldn't break a 45-degree angle.

She got 13 feet 9 inches. And she was ecstatic about

it. Nobody has tried to beat her record since she set it on October 9, 2021.

My heart could have exploded watching her celebrate her accomplishment with her friends while playing on the water slide. At Valentina's. It came full circle for me at that moment. It was the single greatest day of my life. She was so happy. Standing in front of a building named after her. All the sacrifices really paid off that day.

Valentina's was winning so many awards. We were making more money. We had a great brand, a wonderful product, and people waited for an hour to have pizza at Valentina's during the week. Nobody cared about the location.

Meanwhile, I brought in a young woman who had a law degree, who was looking for a server job for extra money. I hired Camryn on the spot. It didn't take her long to start to impress me. She was detailed, sharp, smart, and I trusted her. I gave her more administrative duties and more hours.

Valentina's started running like a machine. I had ten employees. And I was able to lean into my own personal growth and start looking at what I wanted more of in my future. To help guide me through personal and professional development, I hired a life coach for the first time. We met at the gym, and I was immediately impressed with his background. He was retired military with a background in tactical warfare in the air force.

He and I started mapping out what I really wanted in life. We worked together several times a week, and after a while, I started offering his services to my staff. I saw the benefits of Brian in my life. My high-school sweetheart became my girlfriend. After thirty years of not asking her on a date, I finally asked her to come to Alabama.

The business improved. And my relationship with Valentina, her mom, and her stepdad all improved.

A friend of mine with a good head for business came into Valentina's one day when we were packed. He encouraged me to think bigger.

"Joe, you have to think beyond this little space or you'll start losing business because you can't even get into the parking lot on a Tuesday," he said.

He told me about a piece of property no more than 500 feet away from where we were. It was an empty lot.

"Call my banker and set up a meeting," he said.

I listened to him and got a meeting a few days later. And like many times before, I poured my guts out. I put it all on the table. I was up front about the fact that my credit was probably shit but Valentina's was going to make it. We needed a bigger space.

"Let me see your numbers. That's all that matters," the banker said.

I sent him everything he needed and then went to the Pizza Expo in Las Vegas in March 2022. While competing, I won the Best Traditional Pizza in the World, and Valentina's blew up in the press. We were everywhere, and so were customers. We had longer lines than ever before. It didn't take the banker long to call me.

"You got approved, Joe," he said.

"You sure?" I laughed?

"Hell yeah. You've got it."

I didn't waste time calling my high school sweetheart

to share the news. She was so excited for me, and while we hadn't seen each other in person, we were growing closer together. It was nice to have her as a champion in my life again.

My next call was to the man who owned the property. He was willing to sell it to me on one condition: He was a builder, and to own the land, I had to let him build the pizzeria.

"Have you ever built a restaurant before?" I asked him.

"No, but it's not any different than building a house," he said.

"Really?" I laughed.

"It's a pre-fabricated metal building. You tell me the measurements; it gets built off-site and shipped to be put up on your property."

"Okay, let me think about it and I'll give you a call tomorrow," I said.

Dozens of thoughts spun through my mind at once. People were already driving out of their way to come to Valentina's. The ones who loved my place would get why I wanted to build something from the ground up, and bigger to support the growth everyone saw for me. I was taking a chance on new fans driving out of the way for pizza.

Taking a leap of faith wasn't new to me. I'd been doing it forever. But I knew in my gut I was about to embark on a nightmare. The builder lacked restaurant experience, but I felt trapped. The property was in a great location. It wasn't perfect though.

The land was in Limestone County, and from what I heard, the county was the wild west, except without booze.

The county was dry. Valentina's sat on one side of the street, with a bar inside, and where I wanted to buy land and build out our future was on the opposite side of the street, with no booze. The trade-off, according to the builder and everyone I spoke to, was that there were no rules. I was told I wouldn't need permits, so I assumed up to that point, I could build what I wanted, where I wanted, and how I wanted it.

The builder told me that he hated dealing with the city. To build a restaurant in the city, I needed a permit for plumbing, walls, electrical, and even to build a foundation. To do anything and everything, I needed a different permit.

The county, though, was a different story. They didn't care about permits.

"The county is the way to go. And I'll make sure everything is up to code, but I am not going to deal with any permits. That was on you," the builder said.

I was told I'd have to annex Huntsville City with an easy application.

It's a smooth process. No big deal. Easy peasy.

I didn't need the night to sleep on it. I knew I was going to ignore the red flag, bite the bullet, and move forward. I called the builder at eight a.m. the next morning and told the owner to send me over a contract, and I'd have my team review it.

It took a few weeks to finalize our agreement between our legal teams. And once it was signed, I drove to the bank, got a check for $30,000, and drove it to his home personally. It was early spring. I had the windows cracked and took a deep breath before walking up to his front door.

"Let's get going," I said when I handed over his money.

A few days later, I got a call from the builder, and he told me to go out and measure the property and tell him the size of the building I wanted.

Building out a restaurant was a new experience in my life. I had never built anything from the ground up. More than that, nobody in the World Pizza Champions had been down this path before. I was on my own here. Tony hadn't even built something from scratch before.

I called up my friend and mentor from The Arsenal and asked him to meet me at the property. He was the only person I knew who had ever built a building from the ground up. He met me with a walking measuring wheel. And we measured out the building together.

My mentor asked about the annexation process and where we were with it even before we finished measuring the build out.

"I asked about it last week and the lady I spoke to laughed about it and said build it first and we'll annex after," I said.

I shrugged, and my mentor nodded his head in agreement. Something didn't feel right, but I didn't know what. Everything was overwhelming and out of my scope.

CHAPTER TWELVE

VALENTINA'S 2.0

TO SAY THAT THE NEW BUILD DIDN'T GO SMOOTHLY IS a flat-out lie—it was a disaster. But I didn't know what I didn't know. What I know now, however, is that it'd be a cold day in hell before I agree to build anything from scratch in a dry county again. And to take it one step further, if I ever say yes to a new build in the future—Valentina's 3.0, for example—I'll do everything differently.

After my mentor and I measured out the land, the builder connected me with a designer. I assumed I only needed one designer. So, I just went along with the meeting set up for me. The designer seemed really nice and knowledgeable. He pulled up what the building would look like on his computer. I was able to see the next version of Valentina's in a 3D rendering through his software system. It was exciting and I wanted to get to the next phase.

Over the next several weeks, the designer and I met again to finalize how I wanted the kitchen built out, where I wanted the bar and how I wanted it to look, where the parking lot would go, and even where the windows should be placed.

As much as I wanted the place to be built and open the instant I signed a contract, it was a slow-moving process.

The building was fabricated. And it took six months to build and ship. The building showed up in October in pieces. There was one flatbed for the framing. And in two days, the metal exterior was put up and built.

Camryn was transitioning out of her career as an attorney and looking for more hours at the pizzeria. I knew I could run a restaurant by myself. I knew my strengths and weaknesses and didn't need a partner, but I did need a sharp manager who understood my vision.

What I still needed help with was communicating with the builder. After the pre-fabricated building went up, I started having issues with the builder's contractors. He didn't have a general contractor on site overseeing Valentina's build-out.

I would show up at the new property and have to change where they were putting outlets, piping, and the level of the bar. Some days, nobody was on the site doing the work that was promised that day. I had anxiety over it all and would get so angry at his employees not showing up.

I knew Camryn could step in as the general contractor of the new build, and she dove in headfirst. She took it and ran with it. I told her what I wanted it to look like. She did it all. She went from being a server to a general contractor. Promoting her was a no-brainer to me.

She was amazing at managing the new build, the permits, the city officials, the contracts, and all the moving parts.

Even though we had a designer draw up plans, a designer

plan for a new build is not the same as an architectural plan, and without one of those, we were screwed. Every time we needed to add an outlet, we had to change the work order, which cost $300 a pop. And we did that at least 30 times.

Every time the builder needed something picked out, I'd get a text to make a decision.

What door frames do I want? What shade of brick? What lightning fixture? What color outlet?

It was a lot of work, on top of a lot of work. We were still in full operation at the original store. And thank God for Camryn. I'd make a decision, and she'd run to pick up everything and anything we needed just to help save on delivery charges. She made brick runs, lightning fixture runs, all while still doing her day job as my manager. I don't know how anyone can do a new build while operating a pizzeria without help.

We had an Excel spreadsheet of everything that had to be ordered. Camryn had every area of the pizzeria organized on different spreadsheet tabs, and what we needed in each area listed on each tab.

- Entry Room
- Bourbon Room
- Dining Room
- Bar Area
- Server Stations
- Pizza Line
- Kitchen
- Bathroom
- Dish Pit
- Dry Storage Room
- Office
- Patio
- Break Room
- Outside
- Misc

We were going from 1,000 square feet to 4,000 square feet so even though we had pizza stands and kitchenware, we needed a ton more of it.

In the Bar Area alone, we needed to order and budget for:

- Seating
    - Bar Stools (10 inside)
    - Bar Stools (10 outside)
- Tools/Utensils
    - Bottle Opener
    - Wine Opener
    - Cocktail Napkins
    - Jigger
    - Ice Tong
    - Bourbon Ice Tray
    - Phone
    - POS
    - Coke Gun
- Build Out
    - Bar Tops
    - Wine Fridge (2)
    - Beer Cooler (Bottles)
    - Beer Cooler (Keg)
    - Dishwasher
    - Ice Machine
    - Shelving
    - Foot Rail
    - Bag Hooks

In the Dining Room, we needed to order and budget for:

- Main Room
    - Tables (15)
    - Chairs (80)
    - Pizza Stands
    - Shakers
    - Decor (Pictures for the walls)

In the Server Section, we needed and had to budget for:

- Storage Area
    - Counter Build (2)
    - Coke Machine (2)
    - POS (2)
    - Handheld (2)

The back of the house was done first, so we had furniture delivered for the office and break room. To staff a 4,000-square-foot pizzeria, I was going to have to hire more help. I wanted to create a place where people could have careers and love coming to work. I wanted Valentina's to be a place where people could earn a good living, spend quality time with their families, and stay for life if they wanted.

To achieve that, I knew I'd have to invest in their mental health and shower them with as much love and support as I could while they were working. I imagined we'd need at least 50 staff members when we were running at full speed.

I gave my vision of the break room to Camryn and let her order and budget for:

- Break Room
    - Espresso machine
    - Slushie machine
    - Couch (2)
    - Blankets (4)
    - Pillows (4)
    - Snacks and beverages.

We could finally have the equipment delivered when the kitchen was built out. However, I did have to get another loan for equipment, such as kitchen cooking tools, eating utensils, and glasses.

And the kitchen was what we had to order the most for.

- Serveware:
    - Garlic Knot Basket
    - Appetizer Bowl
    - Small Cheese Board
    - Large Cheese Board
    - Appetizer Plate
    - Salad Plate
    - Paleo Bowl
    - Circle Pizza Bowl

    - Detroit Pans
    - Sicilian Pans
    - Pizza Spatulas
    - Calzone Plates
    - Dessert Plates
    - Dessert Boards
- Flatware
    - Dinner Forks (400)
    - Dinner Knives (400)
    - Dessert Spoons (200)
- Dinnerware
    - Appetizer/Dessert Plates (400)
    - Dinner Plates (400)
- Glassware
    - Drinking Glasses (400)
    - Beer Glasses (250)
    - Wine Glasses (250)
    - Bourbon Glasses (200)
- Tools/Utensils
    - Measure Cups
    - Measuring Spoons
    - Prep Knives
    - Scoops
    - Tongs
    - Graters
    - Whisks
    - Thermometer Freezers
    - Thermometer Fryers
    - Thermometers
    - Pastry Brushes

We arranged for supplies to be delivered little by little, so it wasn't pure chaos. But because the new build took so much longer than we anticipated, we also couldn't sit on our asses and let long periods of time go by before the next delivery arrived. It wasn't easy. But the morning our oven was being installed was a day from hell.

It was our dinner rush, and I was on the pizza line in the original store. A friend of ours was trying to get the new oven into the new store without my knowledge. Camryn was at the new store and watched our friend remove the oven from the truck with a forklift. Sadly, the oven fell off the lift, and our friend tried to stop it and accidentally stepped on a nail. It went from a really promising day to the worst one in a matter of minutes. I ran to help the delivery driver, knowing the oven was ruined. There wasn't anything I could do about that. Camryn went right into manager mode and called up the insurance company to see what could get covered.

Nada. Zip.

They didn't help me pay for this poor guy's medical bills or a second oven.

We were a month out from our soft launch, my oven was broken in our parking lot, and I was just hit over the head with unexpected bills. Pizza ovens take months to build, and we didn't have the time to wait for another one. I called up the owner of the pizza oven company, preparing to plead my case. I was hoping for a miracle.

While I waited for the owner to pick up the phone, I prayed and prayed for a blessing. I felt like I was pleading my case to God as well.

I had such a great relationship with the oven company and wasn't ashamed to lay it all out on the line.

The anxiety.

The weight and pressure of tripling in size. Going from debt-free to a massive loan.

Having to hire more help before sales come in. The unexpected medical bill.

And my broken oven.

I didn't have to wait more than a second for my vendor to put me as ease. If there was ever a stereotypical Italian thing to ever happen to me, it was that conversation because my vendor said, "Forget about it."

The next thing I knew, he sent me a purchase order for a brand new oven that was being expedited over in three weeks.

I could have curled up and cried. Tears formed in my eyes. I shut them and squeezed them so tight. I pushed my thumb and index finger in the corners of my eyes to prevent tears from coming out. I felt so much emotion swell up in my chest and sit in a ball in my throat. I forced myself to swallow hard, exhale, and pour out so much gratitude for my friend.

"Man, I can't thank you enough for that. Are you sure? Can you really do that?"

I accepted it the best I could, looked up into the sky, and thanked God before hanging up. That conversation was one of the few wins of the entire new build. And it happened after I thought we'd have to push back our opening. It gave me the boost I needed to keep on going. The kindness of that one man refueled my spirit and twisted my head back on straight.

God blessed us in all our chaos. If I could think clearly in that time of my life, I'd be able to say it was always like that. I saw blessings come out of the chaos.

Once the oven was installed, I finally felt like I saw the light at the end of the tunnel. There wasn't much more that had to get done or installed. Or at least, that's what I thought.

Since we were almost done with everything, we started the annex paperwork with the city on a Monday.

"Well, everything seems to be in order," the lady said on the phone.

Easy peasy.

I kept the momentum going by reaching out to the right person to get our liquor license in motion.

Bam.

Getting a liquor license for my pizzeria technically built in a dry county, but in the process of being accepted by the city, was the easiest part of the whole process. And by that point, I needed more easy tasks to check off the long running list of things to get done before we were actually open to the public. I was eager to finish the new build, open the doors, and start making some money.

The weight of the loans I took out to build from the ground up felt heavier and heavier the closer we got to the opening. I was using every free minute I had to work out my stress and frustration in the gym. If I wasn't there, I was hanging out with Valentina.

I was so grateful she was witnessing everything personally. She had seen me struggle so badly and had been there with me from the start of the original place. Watching her walk around the new build, three times the size of the original, brought tears to my eyes time and time again.

I was doing all of it for her. It was hers. Whether she was going to take it over for me decades down the road was never discussed. But I made sure she was taken care of. The place was put in her name. She was the landowner. And nobody could ever take this place away from her. I was going to see to it.

I finally thought things were in order and turning around. But everything changed again on Tuesday when the fire marshal walked in as my buddy was hanging up speakers and yelled, "What's all this?"

The fire marshal had our annex paperwork on his desk, and he expected to walk into a restaurant that looked different from my pizzeria. A pizzeria does not have the same elements as a restaurant. And when he didn't see a hood over the oven, he freaked out.

The next day, there was a big sign on the front door of the new place that ordered all work to stop until further notice.

My heart sank as I held the notice in my hand. I called Camryn and asked her to get down to the new store right away. I couldn't believe how close we were to finishing the build out and at the very last minute, we're stopped in our tracks.

Everything felt like it fell apart that morning. I was angry and frustrated. It felt like the left hand was the county and the right hand was the city and no matter how many times we called, we couldn't get the two connected.

Later that day, the fire marshal came by again. But this time, he brought out seven different inspectors. They're looking at electrical, plumbing, and equipment inside and outside the building. And I lost my mind.

I screamed at the fire marshal. Absolutely lost my shit on him. "We're grandfathered in!" I yelled.

He wasn't having any of it. He listed off a crap-ton of things that had to be adjusted right there on the spot.

- The toilet has to move a half-inch
- Door frames
- Different lights

The more he spat at me, the angrier I got. Camryn kept

her cool. She was the good Southern Charm to my hot-tempered New York, and in that moment, those Southern men didn't want anything to do with me.

"Go outside, Joe," Camryn said.

I was so pissed I didn't hear her the first few times she said it. But I got it when she stepped right in front of my face, gritted her teeth, and said it sternly. I got it. I stormed outside and took myself on a walk, trusting Camryn was going to charm those guys and fix that mess.

It took a while for my temper to regulate. I thought back to all the other times in my life, when something that was mine was ripped out from underneath me. Unfairly. Because of my own ego. Pride. But this time was different. We went through the proper channels. We followed the guidance we were given. I didn't fuck it up.

The faster I walked, the clearer my head got. I had been through enough lessons in my life to know how to have a calm conversation with someone about my business. I turned around, walked into Valentina's 2.0, apologized for my outburst and storming out, and introduced myself to the fire marshal, deputy director, and the rest of the inspectors who were there.

Camryn smiled at me, watching me and the others. I'm sure she was nervous, but I had my emotions under control. Over the next twenty minutes, I told them all the whole story of how we got to where we were at that moment.

The fire marshal was a hard man. He wasn't easily moved. But the deputy director seemed to be on our side.

But when they all left, we were told we had a list of things to fix, and they'd be back in a month.

Later that day, I got this email letting me know all the things I had to change before I could open to the public.

Building Code:

1. **The building is currently not non-sprinklered.** A reduction to this proposed OL was requested per the owner so to have the main building OL to under 100-OL. The owner suggested removal of all or part of the existing type VB construction on the side outdoor covered seating area. Also, per owner's request for an option to have a licensed Alabama fire protection engineer to review the current building for an alternative design approach and approval. The current building construction per architectural plan was noted as a type IIB construction, per onsite inspection the construction type was determined to be a type VB construction. This was due to interior load bearing wood framed walls for the kitchen and other interior divided areas with a sheetrock hard lid ceiling supported by wood ceiling joist. The architectural plans will need to be revised to correct these noted changes and reflect the new proposed occupant load showing any new revisions.
2. Both bathrooms are noted as not meeting ADA requirements with the following items needing to be addressed; water closets are too close to the side wall, water closet needs an open front seat, grad bars are too high from finish floor level, current install laboratories are not accessible for height and knee space clearances, no current ADA faucet was installed with lever type controls. Both

bathroom doors need automatic closing devices installed. The reinstallation of the plumbing fixtures must be per 2018 IPC.

3. Emergency e-lights are required above the electrical panel location and also at each exit door on the discharge side of the door.
4. Limestone County Health Department final approval is needed for food service permit.

Electrical Code:

1. The existing electrical service is a 3-phase 120/208volt. A load calculation is needed to verify that the service is not overloaded.
2. Improper feeder conductor was installed from the exterior disconnect to the interior panel. The conductors used (USE-2) are only rated for exterior underground use. This needs to be replaced with a code compliant feeder conductor and sizing accordingly for the load and service condition. The current installed conductors are not phased correctly and need to be properly installed when changed.
3. All service conductors must be properly torqued to manufactures/NFPA 70 specifications. The existing conditions at the main disconnect are noted as not being torqued properly and therefore the required manufactured installed arch-flash shielding are not currently installed properly due to this reason. Address as noted.
4. Verification of product testing & listings is needed for all the existing custom lighting fixtures used in the building.

5. Remove onsite site-built pole light fixtures used in the restrooms to a listed type of fixture.
6. All single-phase receptacles rated 150 volts to ground or less, 50 amperes or less and three phase receptacles rated 150 volts to ground or less, 100 amperes or less installed in the following locations shall have ground-fault circuit-interrupter protection for personnel. Kitchen, bathroom, indoor wet locations and outdoors must be GFCI protected.
7. Install proper GFCI circuits for the new pizza oven.

Mechanical & Gas Code:

1. A proper float switch needs to be installed at each air handler unit located in the attic on the auxiliary drain pan and must be connected to the associated unit.
2. The existing HVAC system is currently installed without any fresh air ventilation being introduced into the building and/or installed to the HVAC units as required per the 2018 IMC. The installed HVAC system/equipment must be evaluated for the required amounts of fresh air and must be revised to meet the adopted 2018 IMC for proper indoor air quality and ventilation design per ASHRAE 62.1.
3. A platform and walkway to the attic mechanical units will be required to be installed. COH code as listed COH adopted code change—306.3 Appliances in attics to be accessible" to read:

"All appliances in attics must be accessible and meet the requirements as found in the definition of Readily Access (To). Attics containing appliances shall be provided with an opening and unobstructed passageway large enough to allow removal of the largest *appliance*.

The passageway shall be not less than 30 inches (762 mm) high and 22 inches (559 mm) wide and not more than 20 feet (6096 mm) in length measured along the centerline of the passageway from the opening to the *appliance*. The passageway shall have continuous solid flooring not less than 24 inches (610 mm) wide. A level service space not less than 30 inches (762 mm) deep and 30 inches (762 mm) wide shall be present at the front or service side of the *appliance*. The clear access opening dimensions shall be not less than 20 inches by 30 inches (508 mm by 762 mm), and large enough to allow removal of the largest *appliance*.

1. Proper clearance required at each attic HVAC air handler from the class B exhaust vent to all combustible material.
2. The onsite gas piping looked to be under sized for a low-pressure system based on the installed appliance and total BTUH ratings. Verification of the existing installation is required to determine if the low-pressure system is large enough for the total loading. Options to change to a high pressure system of a 2psi system will need to be evaluated as well and changed /installed as required per COH local amended 2018 II Fuel Gas Code.
3. Copper tubing was noted being installed from the exterior of the building to interior, concealed in the front exterior wall to two outdoor gas lanterns. This portion of gas tubing was also noted as using improper compression-type fittings. This portion of the gas piping needs to be replaced or removed. If replaced, then the piping material and

installation used must be installed. Retesting the system will be required. Cooper/copper alloy tubing for gas piping is only allowed to be used interior of a building in COH, between rigid piping and the appliance and not concealed.

Plumbing Code:

1. Insulate all water piping in the enclosed attic space per 2018 IPC to protect against possible freezing conditions, since this area is an unconditioned space.
2. Reinstallation of any plumbing fixture due to ADA compliance must be reinstalled to meet the 2018 IPC.
3. Label /ID both bathrooms with proper signage noting ADA compliant with braille per ICC ANSI A117.1 2009.

I didn't understand most of it or even know where to start. Luckily, we had great relationships with enough people in town by that point, and all I had to do was make a few phone calls, and folks started showing up to address these issues.

One by one, I got them checked off the list. Meanwhile, Camryn put her attorney cap back on and read through the code book. She wanted to be totally prepared for whatever these guys were going to throw at us again, if anything. She called to get another inspection scheduled and the soonest the fire marshal agreed to come back out was on the morning of our Friends and Family Day.

I hadn't rescheduled anything. I was holding onto faith and praying like hell, it was all going to turn out okay. But, I admit, if the final inspection could have happened at any other point, I would have preferred that. That was cutting it close even for me—the guy who drove out to competitions the night before, slept in his car, and drove back home before work in the morning.

The morning of December 10, 2023, came, and Camryn and I were waiting in the dining room for them all. Right on time, a truckload of people came back out. I looked at her, and she looked ready. She had the original list in one hand and the code printed out in the other.

All my nerves relaxed. I knew she was going to handle this one like an attorney, not a general manager who served as a general contractor.

We welcomed everyone inside, shaking everyone's hand. There were seven inspectors again.

Camryn had her southern charm cranked up to a 12. I kept my New Yorker front and center but let her take the lead. The fire marshal and a few other inspectors started walking around. The deputy director wasn't there, and he was the one guy we wanted there the most.

I saw Camryn pull up his phone number on her phone and keep it ready. Just then, the fire marshal started listing out new things for us to change, the biggest thing being that he said we were over the square footage for fire sprinklers due to the patio.

Camyrn had her work cut out for her, and I knew just by the look on her face she was about to use her big law degree and her litigating skills. I watched in awe as she respectfully challenged any changes the inspectors made.

"Sir," Camryn said, holding out the document she had printed out with the city code on it. "I called and discussed this with a staff member of yours. The code is not written very well. It's very grey. Your staff member said that whether or not you approve of us will depend on your mood on the day you inspect us. So, I'm counting on you being in a great mood today, sir, considering this code is not laid out well, and we did call to discuss it."

I held back my smirk but was celebrating inside.

"That woman should not have told you that," the fire marshal snapped. "I know who you are speaking of, and she was let go."

"Well, even so, sir, we are within what the code states."

The fire marshal was having a hard time letting this go. It seemed more like we offended him by not including him in the buildout from the start. That wasn't something I could change since I was expecting our friends to show up in eight hours for pizza. So, I said the only thing I thought was going to move us forward.

"I don't mean to pour gas on the fire here, but you do know she's an attorney, right?" The fire marshal looked at me and then at Camryn.

"Here is the list you gave us to correct, sir," she said. "This has all been updated."

Pointing out her law background didn't piss him off, but it didn't stop him either. He said we had the day to prove to him that if there was a fire in the building, anyone and everyone could get out of Valentina's safely with just a fire alarm and not a fire sprinkler system.

I had the day to find a fire safety inspector, get him out to the shop, have him review our place, menu, and layout, come up with a plan, and get it approved by the fire marshal.

All in a matter of hours. As luck would have it, there was a fire safety inspector who was free. That day. I could hear my heart pounding in my ears as I gave him the address. Things felt like they were working out for our good. I knew in my bones that everything was going to be okay.

I gave Camryn a thumb's up. She called the deputy director to get him to sign off on the rest of the list. Not long after, the inspector showed up. He looked over the equipment, did a walkthrough, met with the fire marshal and an hour later, the fire marshal signed off on Valentina's with one exception. If I ever sell the building, the fire marshal wouldn't transfer it to someone else.

Hours later, we opened our doors to our friends and family and welcomed everyone inside the new and improved Valentina's.

In hindsight, for industry folks interested in building from the ground up...

The builder tried to build the pizzeria as a big house. I'd know the next build-out would be much easier. Get an architect, get a designer, call the city, get them involved right away, invite them out to meet in person, and walk them through the property. City codes can be poorly written and very grey. Budget. Know the cost. Know your value. Make it make sense for you. Get a GC if you've never done this before. Different materials get dirty faster, different shades work better with different lighting, and various exteriors work better with different weather. The flow of your kitchen matters.

CHAPTER THIRTEEN

THE BEST OF THE BEST

I HAD MIXED FEELINGS WHILE STANDING IN THE NEW Valentina's that day. I was grateful for all Camryn did to ensure those inspectors did not spoil our big launch. But on the other hand, I was standing in a massive space praying that more people would fill it.

On the outside, I hoped I looked cool and calm. But my mind raced one thousand miles per hour that night.

The next day, we were open to the public.

Building a store from scratch wasn't the only stressful element of the new location. In the first Valentina's, I didn't have a loan. I was saving more money than ever before. I had eight, sometimes ten, employees at the first location. And at the second location, everyone on staff was working as much as they possibly could. It wasn't easy.

We wanted a full staff of fifty to help with the demand, but we couldn't find people right away. We tried. Being next to a cornfield and a subdivision doesn't make it easy to find employees. We're out in the middle of nowhere. Getting a specific mindset and expertise in the perfect candidate was a tall order.

Throughout 2024, we were gratefully able to grow our staff little by little. As we grew, we had to make sure everyone was a perfect fit for us—our family. I gave Camryn the reins on our personal growth. I stayed out of it. She was able to grow our internal family from 10 to 50 within a year.

Something I learned along the way was to invest in my staff. With my daughter's name on the building, I knew I wasn't making any of the same mistakes as I did in the past. I invested in my own personal growth, and as I started to see changes in my life, personal and professional, I offered my staff opportunities to meet with my life coach, Brian Robinson. And he was the best investment I ever made in my staff. He offered his help several times a week to our staff to support any hiccups or arguments, so personal challenges never showed up on the dining room floor. Our most significant growth challenge was getting 50 different personalities to work well together. Still, Brian, Camyrn, and I worked together to ensure the back-of-the-house ran like a machine. And a strong culture is shown in the product. They all take ownership of what we put out on the tables.

During 2024, Brian helped us establish leadership development and helped us select specific candidates to promote.

When I started to stress or get worked up, I would take a step away from everyone and collect my thoughts for a few beats. I'd remind myself of the fact that we had to move. We outgrew the first location. We made one million in sales in one year. And I wanted so much more for Valentina.

Stress was present a lot. Mostly because I was a landlord. My daughter was a landlord. I made sure I set up Valentina's lease to support my daughter long after I was done with it. The blessing was that I work exceptionally hard and I'm great under pressure. And that's because of my ADHD. And I depended on my ability to work hard under pressure.

Before we opened the new location, Camryn and I sat down to discuss the type of culture I wanted among the staff. This industry is hard enough without personal drama in the back of the house—and drama among the staff.

Camryn was like a rock for me during that time in life, and before we knew it, it was time for the next International Pizza Expo in Las Vegas.

There are moments in life when time slows down—not because things get easier, but because everything I sacrificed finally found its purpose. For me, that moment came at the International Pizza Expo 2024 because I was competing for a title I had chased for more than two decades.

The only competition I could enter that year was the Best of the Best World Pizza Champion. The Best of the Best competition is an invite-only competition consisting of competitors who have won Pizza Maker of the Year in prior years.

At the previous International Pizza Expos, I won:

- 2022 Best Traditional Pizza in the World;
- 2023 Best Non-Traditional Pizza in the World;
- 2023 Pizza Maker of the Year.

The Best of the Best was my last chance to impress judges who saw the best from around the world. But for me, it wasn't just about ingredients or timing—it was about redemption.

I'd been competing for over 25 years, but that year, I competed like never before. I was tired of always being close to winning. Sometimes inches from the podium. But never quite enough. I watched others win while I walked away empty-handed, year after year. Each time, I carried the weight home with me—the doubt, the disappointment, the quiet voice inside asking if I was just chasing something I'd never catch. But I never quit. I couldn't.

Because I wasn't just showing up and competing for me anymore. I was doing it to show my daughter what it meant to keep fighting for what you love. I always told her: "Never give up. Never let the opinions of others define your worth." And that year, I had to live that truth on the biggest stage in our industry.

Before the competition, I reached out to a judge who had once critiqued my work years earlier. She was warm, honest, and real. After losing the Pizza Maker of the Year title two years before, I had walked straight up to her and asked, "What do I need to do to get better?" That one conversation lit a fire in me. The following year, I won my division—and then, against the odds, I took Pizza Maker of the Year. The first ever to win back-to-back divisions and then claim the title. That was history. But it still wasn't enough.

Best of the Best was the final chapter.

I prepped like no one else. And, unlike everyone else, I took my dough preparation to a different level. The only thing pizza competitors are allowed to bring into a competition is our dough.

I made my dough in my Alabama kitchen before leaving for Las Vegas. I put it on ice on the plane and booked a private hotel room just for my dough to rest. And for me to rest as well—a controlled environment in a hotel room, away from the chaos of the competition. No walk-ins, no cooler blasts, no distractions. Just focus. Just respect for the process. I stayed in a separate room and monitored the temperature to the degree. Every variable mattered.

The Best of the Best competition could have been an episode of Chopped. We all received a surprise basket of ingredients we had to use. In the basket were red onion, pork belly, and pineapple.

When I saw the ingredients, my mind immediately flashed back to something a judge had told me the year before: "Keep it simple." That advice stayed with me. It would've been easy to overcomplicate the dish or try to show off. But instead, I took a risk in a different direction—I focused on balance. And I added one unexpected twist: fresh mint.

Mint was a curveball. It could have elevated the dish or completely thrown off the profile, but I trusted my instincts.

I caramelized the pineapple to enhance its natural sweetness and deepen the flavor. I diced and roasted the pork belly in the wood-fired oven on site, letting it crisp and render to perfection. I chose a red sauce base—a decision that some might have second-guessed—but it made sense to me. The sweetness and tang of the pineapple worked against the acidity and richness of the tomato sauce, cutting through the fat and refreshing the palate. The red onions brought just the right bite to pull it together.

When the pizza was done, I topped it with a julienned touch of mint. That final touch made the flavor deeper—something personal.

I wasn't alone that day. My World Pizza Champion teammates were there, cheering me on. So was my team from Valentina's. Even an old friend from high school—there for business, not pizza—showed up to support me.

When it was finally time to present pizza to the judges, I went last. I wanted the quiet, the stillness, and the judges to feel the gravity of the moment.

I built a presentation that stood out before the first bite—flowers around the plate, colors, and textures designed to pull their eyes and their emotions toward the experience. And then, I stepped forward and gave the most honest speech of my life:

> "My dough has been in a separate hotel room all week, carefully watched and protected. I wanted to make sure that when you try this pizza, you're not just tasting food—you're tasting a piece of me. Because like pizza, and like life, I am always evolving.
>
> I'm always trying to be better.
> A better father.
> A better boss.
> A better pizzaiolo.
> A better friend.
> A better son.
> A better brother.
> A better boyfriend.
>
> That's what this pizza represents. My growth. My journey. My commitment to this craft—and to life."

I spoke as they tried my red sauce-based pizza with mozzarella, seared pork belly, caramelized pineapple, red onions, topped with mint.

When I finished talking, there was a pause. Not from doubt—but from impact. That silence was louder than applause.

I watched them take bites and lift the pizza to check out the crust. I answered questions about my cooking process and then left the judges to deliberate. I sat down in the audience section, next to Camryn, and prayed.

God, please let this be over. I'm ready for closure. I've done my best. Please let it be enough this time.

The judges made their decision after a few minutes, and then the winners were announced in the order in which they competed. Since I was in the very last competition, I had to wait another half hour before I finally found out my fate.

When they announced *Joe Carlucci* as the Best of the Best winner, everything hit me at once. I clapped my hands around my head and jumped around, hugging friends nearby. But internally, my mind was flooded with memories where I came up short. Flashbacks of times I nearly walked away. I got quick images of people who said I wasn't ready. Every time I questioned if this was still worth chasing.

My emotions were on another level. I thought of my daughter and the promises I made her—about grit, about grace, about never quitting. And I had lived it. All of it. Right there, on that stage.

After the announcement, I looked over and saw one of the most meaningful faces in my life—my longtime mentor, Tony. He just smiled and said, "You earned it." And that hit me differently.

But maybe the most powerful moment came afterward, when I found the judge who had once given me the advice that changed everything. She walked straight up to me, wrapped me in a huge hug, smiled, and said, "See what happens when you listen?"

She's now become a close friend and mentor, an Iron Chef judge, an author, and a restaurateur—a woman who helped me see what I needed to become.

Having my team—my General Manager, my lead pizza maker, and my niece—there with me made the moment even more fulfilling. These competitions took a lot out of me. When I came up short, it wore on me. I was used to walking away, questioning myself, my abilities, and my direction. I was familiar with leaving empty-handed. But when I finally won this one, every single loss became worth it. I got my icing on the cake.

I've learned that anything is possible if you stay open to change, if you stay humble and listen.

The Best of the Best competition is unlike anything else. You can't prepare a full routine in advance. You don't bring your toppings; your own layout. You bring one thing—your dough. That's it. The rest? You have to adapt on the fly, with no hesitation. If you freeze up, it's over.

The competitors are no joke. It's made up of the past four winners of Pizza Maker of the Year. This time, it was two Italians, me, and another incredible pizzaiolo. And beating the Italians? I'll never forget it.

Not because I beat them—but because I earned their respect that day. That meant more to me than any title.

There's a quiet skepticism that some of the Italian legends carry toward American pizza makers. They don't always see us as equals. But that day, I felt them look at me differently. I saw it in their eyes. That moment—that respect—is something I will carry for the rest of my life.

Best of the Best wasn't just a title. It was proof. Proof that if you put your heart in the dough, your soul in the process, and your story on the plate, someone will love it.

I made history in 2024. I was named Best of the Best and the first person in history to place three years in a row.

It took me a few weeks to process what happened, especially because after Tony congratulated me, he reminded me that I could never compete at the Pizza Expo again. I had won every single title that I could win, and it was time to move on from competing there.

I looked at that as more of a challenge than anything else.

This is my time.

It felt like I was staring down a clock. I pictured myself with only so many more hours left to really succeed and garner attention. I put everything on black and went all out on press and marketing angles. I hired a publicist to get me national press opportunities, podcast opportunities, and introduce me to producers looking for reality show content.

Two months later, Valentina and I were standing backstage at the Sherri Shepherd Show, talking with another guest that day—Donny Wahlberg. Never in a million years could I have pictured things unfolding that way.

Valentina and I had the time of our lives. We had an amazing segment with Sherri, and then we played a pizza game against Sherri and Donny. It was a quick trip to New York and back, and we saw a great boost in sales after the show aired.

Two months later, Camryn and I were back in New York to accept the biggest award a pizzeria could receive. There are just under 75,000 pizzerias in the United States. And every year, there is a list of the Top 50 Pizzerias in the United States. The list is created by a bunch of Italian inspectors. Nobody knows who the inspectors are. I don't know when they were in Valentina's. But being named the 31st best pizzeria in the country in 2024 was by far the highest honor I received.

Placing within the top 50 best pizzerias in the country puts Valentina's in a category among the best of the best. This is a total testament to my amazing team and the hard work they put into Valentina's day in and day out. We wouldn't have been ranked if it weren't for all of them.

As soon as we got back from that trip, I found out we were named Best Pizzeria in *Alabama Magazine.* That was mind-blowing because it was voted upon by fans. Readers. Residents. It wasn't just people who knew how to make good pizza. It was voted upon by people who ate good pizza.

Later that year, we received the Best Hospitality Award from the Huntsville Chamber of Commerce.

With every story, more customers came. Some would wait in line for an hour. Others would drive four hours. But more and more always came. And I know they weren't coming to meet me. Or the Famous Joe's that they may or may not have ever heard about. But they are coming to a place I put my heart and soul into.

Along with the fans and the pizza lovers came the critics and haters, especially when I used the 2024 presidential campaign in my marketing tactics in November 2024. I knew the marketing angles would be controversial, but I didn't expect the results we saw.

The press ate it up. And it created a splash in more ways than I expected.

While the haters took to review websites to slander and shame, I couldn't have cared less. But I clapped back when they spoke negatively about Valentina or a staff member. Camryn stepped in to help me report false reviews.

But at the end of November, our sales increased by 30%. The staff loved it, too. As more people slammed us online, more people came in to support us, the staff, and me. They were making more money than ever before. I had opportunity after opportunity to stand up for what I believe in, support the country I love, and support my staff.

When Trump won, I came up with a second new box idea. And that one really pissed people off. More and more people took to websites to talk trash, try to bring us down. But the more the haters spoke out about me, Valentina, and our staff, the more support we got. The longer the wait times were at the door. And the best part about it was that the staff couldn't have cared less because it was more money in their pocket.

Valentina trusted I knew what I was doing. She wanted to be at the store, taking it all in, watching what was unfolding for us. And I loved it.

She's seen the struggle. She remembers when I had to sell our furniture to keep the lights on. She's seen the awards and the recognition. And she had even been on national television alongside me.

What I'm most proud of is the man I've grown into

because of Valentina. And because of the pizzeria I named after her, she's grown in her own ways, too.

I'm not the same man, dad, friend, business owner, or World Pizza Champion I was when I started this journey. I might still be a loud New Yorker who will never be considered Southern.

But I found my home. I'm at peace. And I'm ready for what's next.

Where it all began

Valentina is helping her dad on the food truck

Practicing for her Guinness World Record Toss

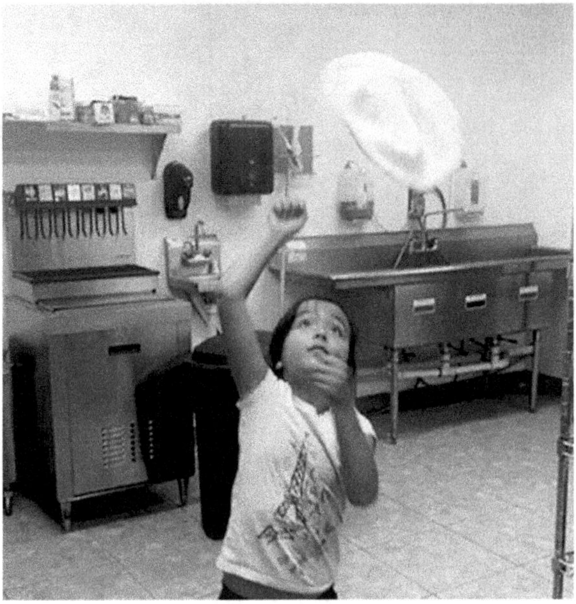

Taken during a photo shoot in our first store.

Winning Pizza Maker of the Year in 2023

The front of the original Valentina's.

Walking out to meet our friends and family, the afternoon we opened Valentina's 2.0 for the first time.

Winning the Best of the Best at the 2024 International Pizza Expo with the expo organizers.

Tossing dough with my daughter.

My heart.

A gratitude letter to my loved ones:

This book would not have been possible without the incredible support, guidance, and belief of so many people who have walked alongside me—both in and out of the kitchen.

First, to my daughter Valentina, whose name graces the front of my pizzeria and whose spirit keeps me grounded and inspired every single day. You are the heart of everything I do.

To my General Manager, Camryn, there are people who walk into your life and change everything—and for me, that person is you. You've been by my side for four years, but it feels like a lifetime of loyalty, grit, and unwavering belief. From day one, you weren't just clocking in; you were showing up—for me, for the team, and for the vision. You didn't just manage a restaurant—you helped build a family. You became *my* family.

Every bit of success I've had over the past four years, every award, every recognition—none of it happens without you. You were there through the grind, through the stress, through the chaos, and the climb. You handled pressure with grace, brought order to madness, and pushed me to be better every single day.

Your fingerprints are on everything we've built. You've helped turn a dream into something real. And the truth is, this journey—this book—doesn't get written without you.

Thank you for being the rock, the engine, the heart of it all. I'm beyond proud to work with you—and even more proud to call you family.

To the entire Valentina's staff, you are family. Your dedication, grit, and passion keep the ovens hot and the customers coming back. I'm beyond proud to work alongside you. Thank you for believing in the vision, showing up every day, and helping make this place what it is: a home, a hustle, and a second chance.

Kory and Julie, I was stepping into the unknown when I moved to Alabama. I came for a job, unsure of what to expect, and a little uncertain about what was ahead. But from the very beginning, you both made me feel like I belonged. You didn't just welcome me — you took me in. You treated me like family, not out of obligation, but out of genuine kindness, compassion, and love. Working for your brother Joe brought me to Alabama, but it was the way you two embraced me that made it feel like home. Whether it was a place to land, a meal to share, or just knowing someone had my back — you were there, always. You supported and encouraged me, never once made me feel like an outsider. Your generosity went beyond anything I expected. You gave without asking for anything in return. You showed me what true hospitality and unconditional support look like, not just in business, but in life. It's something I'll never forget. Thank you for opening your hearts and your home. Thank you for believing in me, standing by me, and treating me like one of your own. I am forever grateful.

To my friend George, some people show up when things are good. But the rare ones—the real ones—stand beside you when you fall flat on your face. You've been that kind of friend to me for over twenty years. You've seen me stumble, fail, and get knocked down more times than I can count—but you never flinched. You never judged. You just stood there, solid, always in my corner. You reminded me of who I was when I forgot. You believed in me when I couldn't see a way forward. And when the world felt heavy, your voice was the one telling me, *"Keep going."*

The truth is, I wouldn't have made it here without that kind of friendship. Without that kind of belief. You gave me the confidence to keep pushing when most would've walked away—and I've never taken that for granted.

Thank you for never giving up on me—even when I was close to giving up on myself. You've been one of the constants in a life full of chaos, and I'll always be grateful for that.

To my brother-in-law, Mike, you've always had my back. Through the highs, the lows, and everything in between—you never doubted me, not once.

When things got tough and people disappeared, you were still there. Still believing in me and still reminding me to keep pushing forward. That kind of support isn't something you find every day. You never made a big deal about it, never asked for anything—you just showed up repeatedly with a good word, a helping hand, and a steady presence when I needed it most.

You were the positive voice in my corner when I felt surrounded by silence. And trust me, that meant more than I ever said out loud. Thank you for being the kind of guy who shows up without needing the spotlight. Thank you for being family in the deepest sense of the word.

To my brother-in-law Joe, thank you for being the one who gave me my first shot in this industry. You opened the door that would eventually become my life's work. I didn't know it back then, but that opportunity was the spark that lit the fire. You believed in me before I knew what I was capable of, and I'll never forget that. Without you, there's no telling where I'd be—but I know I wouldn't be here. Thank you for putting me on this path, seeing something in me, and giving me the chance to chase this dream.

To my cousin Mark, thank you for always being there when things got heavy. You never made a big deal about it—you just showed up with a steady voice, honest advice, and that one phrase that always stuck with me: *"Keep pushing through."* Sometimes I didn't know if I could, but hearing those words from you reminded me that I wasn't alone. You believed in me even when I was struggling to believe in myself. That meant everything. I'm forever grateful for your presence, your heart, and your constant support.

Tony Gemignani, you aren't only my mentor, you are my friend, and my brother. More than 20 years ago, you took me under your wing when I was still trying to find my way. You didn't just show me how to make pizza — you showed me how to carry myself, lead, care about people, and take pride in every detail. You gave me the tools, the confidence, and the values that shaped not only my career but the man I became. You believed in me long before I ever believed in myself. You pushed me, taught me, and stood by me — not just as a teacher, but as family. Without you, none of this would have happened. Without you, there is nothing. Thank you for seeing something in me all those years ago and believing in me when nobody else would.

Thank you, Donatella. After one of my toughest losses, I had the courage to ask you what I could've done better. You didn't just give me advice—you gave me honesty, direction, and your time. That moment could've been brushed off, but instead, it became the beginning of a mentorship I didn't even know I needed.

Since then, you've become more than a mentor—you've become a true friend. You are someone I respect deeply. Someone who's walked the walk and still chooses to lift others up. Your belief in me has meant more than I can put into words. Thank you for always being honest, guiding me without ego, and reminding me that loss is just another step toward greatness.

I want to thank Joe Moore for bringing me to Alabama and believing in me enough to run his restaurant. Your trust, support, and confidence meant the world to me. That opportunity shaped a chapter of my life, for which I'll always be grateful. Without you, there is no Valentina or Valentina's. I will always endeavor to be grateful to you.

Jason Parker, thank you for being a steady guide through the highs and lows of my business journey. Your insight, honesty, and unwavering support helped shape how I lead, grow, and overcome. You didn't just offer advice—you led by example, and that influence helped me build a business I'm proud of. In an industry where things change fast and challenges come even faster, your guidance gave me clarity, confidence, and a sense of direction. I'm grateful for the time, knowledge, and belief you invested in me. This book is a reflection of the business I've built—but it also carries the imprint of those who helped build me along the way. Thank you for being one of them.

To Wisman, for the past 20 years, we've pretty much lived the same life in two different places. We were both grinding in the pizza world, both going through the same ups and downs—not just in business, but in life too. We hit rock bottom, felt the weight of it all, and somehow found a way to climb out.

We talked every day through all of it. Those conversations got me through some of my darkest moments. You always understood because you were living it, too. The advice, the laughs, the real talk—it all mattered. I leaned on those talks more than you know.

Now we're both building something substantial, something real. I look at where we are now, and I know for sure—I wouldn't have made it without you.

Thank you, Derek Sanchez. Your passion for God and pizza is like nothing I've ever seen. It's real. It's deep. And it's contagious. You didn't just talk about dough and fermentation—you helped me *feel* it, understand it, and respect the science behind it. You opened my eyes to a whole new level of this craft, and I'll never look at pizza the same way again.

More than that, you taught, encouraged, and pushed me when I needed it most. You helped put the final pieces together, and because of you, I had the edge to win. You helped me solidify my place, not just in competition, but in my journey. I'm forever grateful for your knowledge, your heart, and your friendship.

To my brothers and sisters in the World Pizza Champions—you've pushed me to be better, faster, sharper. You've shown me that excellence isn't just about the slice, it's about who you become in the process.

Carla, thank you for being there through all of it. From day one, you've had my back—not just during the process of writing this book but throughout the entire journey that led to it.

You saw it all—the stress, the long days, the frustration, the second-guessing. And somehow, you still showed up for me every single time. You never tried to fix it or make it perfect. You just listened, supported, and reminded me to keep going. That meant more than I can ever explain.

This book might have my name on the cover, but the truth is, it wouldn't exist without you. You've been my sounding board, safe space, and biggest supporter. You believed in me, even on the days I didn't believe in myself. I know it hasn't always been easy. But through every late night and every doubt, you never gave up on me. You reminded me of who I am and why I do what I do. Thank you for standing by me, for loving me through the chaos, and for being part of this story—because you're just as much a part of it as I am.

Brian Robinson, my life coach—thank you for helping me keep one foot in the kitchen and the other in the future. Your mentorship has been a game-changer.

Marantha, over the years, we've walked through some of the toughest seasons of life together. We've had our battles—real ones—in court and in life. We've said things we didn't mean, and we've carried hurts that seemed too heavy to ever put down. But somehow, through all of it, we found a way to put the past behind us. We grew up. We grew wiser. And somewhere along the way, we stopped being opponents and became the closest of friends.

We built something I will always be proud of—an unshakable commitment to raising our daughter together. She is the best thing I will ever be a part of, and I take no credit for the incredible person she is becoming. That credit belongs to you. I truly believe, with all my heart, that you are one of the greatest mothers God has ever placed on this earth. My role has always been simple—try not to get in the way of the amazing job you're doing.

In these 12 years, I've watched us both change. We've learned how to listen more, fight less, and keep our focus where it belongs—on loving and guiding our child. And while a lot has shifted over time, one thing has never changed: there is not a single person on this planet who has believed in me more, or cheered louder for me, through every success and every step forward. You've been in my corner when it mattered most, and I will never take that for granted.

From the bottom of my heart, I want to say I am truly sorry for any hurt, stress, or heartache I caused during our rough years. And I also want to say thank you—not just for being an amazing mother, but for being my friend, my supporter, and someone I deeply respect.

We've walked a long road to get here, but I wouldn't trade where we are now for anything. Our daughter has two parents who love her completely, and she gets to grow up seeing what it looks like when people put pride aside and choose to work together. That's a gift we've given her—and I'm proud we gave it together.

To my friend Clay—When I was going through my court battle, you were there. You didn't have to be, and I didn't have to convince you—you just showed up. When I failed in business, you were there again, offering advice, guidance, and the kind of honest mentorship that can only come from a real friend.

In the darkest times, when I felt completely alone—with no family nearby and no friends to turn to—you always found a way to show up. You lifted my spirits when I couldn't lift them myself. For the past 17 years, I've been in Alabama, and you've been a constant in my life.

Now, you've taken on yet another role—my trainer. You care about my health, my business, and my future, not because there's anything in it for you, but because that's just who you are. Your friendship is built on nothing but loyalty, caring, and genuine concern.

I truly appreciate you, Clay. For all the years, all the advice, all the times you've been in my corner—thank you. I'm proud to call you my friend, and I'm even more grateful to have you in my life.

Carrie, when we first connected, it was just supposed to be about PR. You heard my voice, heard how scattered and all over the place I can be, and you never once judged me. From the start, you listened—really listened—to my story. I remember telling you that one day I wanted to write a book about my life, about all the ups, downs, and twists in this crazy journey. You didn't pause, you didn't question—you just said, "Let's do it."

What started a year and a half ago as a simple business arrangement turned into something so much bigger—a lifelong friendship that I truly cherish. Over countless conversations, you've heard me go in every direction possible, my ADHD in full force, and instead of getting frustrated or checking out, you redirected me with patience and care. You have a way of pulling the thread through all my scattered thoughts and tying them together into something that makes sense.

Your talent is unlike anything I've ever seen. You have this rare gift of taking someone's story and not just writing it—but living in it, feeling it, and honoring it. You didn't just write this book; you truly wanted to understand me, to learn where I've been, and to tell it in a way that stayed true to my heart. That's something no amount of skill alone can do—it takes heart, and you have that in abundance.

This book simply wouldn't exist without you. Not because I couldn't have found someone else to write it, but because no one else could have written it like you—because you cared. You didn't just help me tell my story, you helped me find my story. And in doing so, you helped me see pieces of myself I didn't even know were there.

I am beyond proud of this book. But I'm even more proud of what came out of it—our friendship. I now have someone I can call who not only understands my "crazy head" but also accepts it, embraces it, and even helps me make sense of it. You've been my sounding board, my voice of reason, and at times, my mirror when I needed to see myself more clearly.

From the bottom of my heart, thank you—for your talent,

your patience, your belief in me, and most of all, for your friendship. I'm lucky to know you, and I'm even luckier to have you in my life, long after this book is done.

Finally, to every customer who ever believed in the guy who left New York with a temper and a dream: thank you. You helped build more than a business—you helped build redemption.

With deep gratitude,
Joe Carlucci

ABOUT THE AUTHOR

Originally from New York, Joe started in the pizza industry when he was 14 years old, working for his sister's boyfriend's brother's pizzeria, which had ties to "men in suits."

In his 20s, he learned of the pizza competition scene—the World Pizza Games and Tony Gemignani. Joe, Tony, and other chefs traveled the world with choreographed acrobatic pizza-tossing routines. He is a co-founder of the World Pizza Champions, a 501c3 organization that supports pizzeria owners.

Joe was on the Food Network two years in a row, competing against his fellow World Pizza Champions in the first-ever pizza challenge.

In his 30s, after several attempts at running his own business, he took on a pizza consulting gig in Alabama and fell in love with the culture and the people. It became his home. He became General Manager at Tortora's until he opened up another restaurant all his own called Famous Joe's.

Famous Joe's started as a brick-and-mortar. To enhance the business, Joe bought a food truck and eventually got out of the brick-and-mortar and just did the food truck. And then COVID hit and Joe soared.

The food truck community saved Joe. He thrived during COVID, working seven days a week, selling 200 - 300 pizzas a day, just driving 15 miles from his commissary.

In October 2020, he got out of the food truck business and turned the commissary into Valentina's Pizzeria, named after his daughter. The original pizzeria had 40 seats, and they outgrew it within two years.

Joe bought a piece of land 500 feet from the original location and built Valentina's Pizzeria from the ground up at its current location.

Understanding how prominent the burnout culture is in the restaurant industry, Joe created Valentina's as a place that could support families and launch careers, but more importantly, give employees the opportunity to enjoy their lives.

Joe's commitment to his staff is evident in the pride they take in their work. According to the 50 Top Pizza ranking, Valentina's was named the 31st-best pizzeria in the country in 2024 and according to *Alabama Magazine's 2024, 2025 Best of Bama*, it is also ranked as the best pizzeria in Alabama.

He is the 2024 Best of the Best World Pizza Master Champion, the 2023 Pizza Maker of the Year, 2023 International Pizza Expo Winner of Best Non-Traditional Style Pizza in the World, 2022 International Pizza Expo Winner of Best Traditional Style Pizza in the World, a nine-time World Pizza Champion, two-time Guinness World Record Holder, three-time World Champion Pizza Acrobat, and has won awards in competitions worldwide.

He has appeared several times on national TV shows, such as Sherri Shepherd, The Today Show, Martha & Snoop, Master Chef Kids, Best in Dough, and many more. When Joe is not making his world-famous pizza or breaking world records, he is spending time with his daughter and helping her break her own world records.

Find him on Instagram @JoeCarlucci_fj

www.ingramcontent.com/pod-product-compliance
Lightning Source LLC
Chambersburg PA
CBHW062059080426
42734CB00012B/2689
* 9 7 9 8 9 9 9 2 0 5 5 0 6 *